EDUCATIONAL CONFLICT IN THE SUNSHINE STATE

The Story of the 1968 Statewide Teacher Walkout in Florida

DON CAMERON

ROWMAN & LITTLEFIELD EDUCATION
Lanham • New York • Toronto • Plymouth, UK

Published in the United States of America
by Rowman & Littlefield Education
A Division of Rowman & Littlefield Publishers, Inc.
A wholly owned subsidiary of The Rowman & Littlefield Publishing Group, Inc.
4501 Forbes Boulevard, Suite 200, Lanham, Maryland 20706
www.rowmaneducation.com

Estover Road
Plymouth PL6 7PY
United Kingdom

British Library Cataloguing in Publication Information Available

Library of Congress Cataloging-in-Publication Data

Cameron, Don, 1937–
    Educational conflict in the Sunshine State : the story of the 1968 statewide
teacher walkout in Florida / Don Cameron.
        p. cm.
    Includes bibliographical references and index.
    ISBN-13: 978-1-57886-942-8 (cloth : alk. paper)
    ISBN-10: 1-57886-942-0 (cloth : alk. paper)
    ISBN-13: 978-1-57886-943-5 (pbk. : alk. paper)
    ISBN-10: 1-57886-943-9 (pbk. : alk. paper)
    eISBN-13: 978-1-57886-944-2
    eISBN-10: 1-57886-944-7
    1. Collective bargaining—Teachers—Florida.   I. Title.
    LB2842.4.F6C36 2008
    379.759—dc22

                                                                    2008030932

⊗™ The paper used in this publication meets the minimum requirements of
American National Standard for Information Sciences—Permanence of
Paper for Printed Library Materials, ANSI/NISO Z39.48-1992.
Manufactured in the United States of America.

This book is dedicated to the courageous teachers and administrators of Florida who in 1968 risked their jobs and reputations to improve the education of their students.

It is also dedicated to the memory of David Cameron, my brother and staunch supporter of America and public education.

CONTENTS

PREFACE

Few can contest that American public education has been the nation's gateway to greatness. In spite of myriad hurdles placed in its path, public education has succeeded in its mission to educate America's youth. Nine of every ten American citizens—factory workers, farmers, doctors, lawyers, educators, custodians, scientists, and business executives—are products of America's public schools. It is undeniably true that American public education has delivered big time for the public it serves.

It is no less true that financing public education in America can be problematic. Public schools are, after all, totally dependent on funds that emanate from state and local governments that, in turn, derive their resources from the taxes levied on residents of the state. Because of this intrinsically flawed design, there can be a distressing disconnect between what society demands from public education and its willingness to pay for it. One does not have to be an oracle to foresee the adverse correlation between society's mounting expectations for quality education in a global economy and its escalating reticence to increase taxes.

When the public's educational goals conflict with its willingness to pay the tab, stagnation, sometimes severe, can occur. When that happens, education declines and the students and their teachers are adversely affected; and so is society at large. If stagnation devolves to inertia, it can result in open conflict between educators and politicians, as it did in Florida forty years ago.

Truth be told, other than parents, there isn't a societal constituency more intimately connected to students and their needs than teachers. Every day, public school teachers labor in the classrooms, laboratories, gymnasiums, sandboxes, and athletic fields of their charges. Teachers understand firsthand the disparities that sometimes exist between state taxing authorities and the needs of their students, as well as their own needs.

Throughout the nation, no one is more distressed than teachers to live with the absurdity of the richest country on earth allowing millions of its children to be intellectually undernourished because of inadequately funded education programs. Their general distress is magnified greatly when serious education underfunding debilitates their ability to educate their students properly. It was precisely such distress that caused educational darkness to descend on the Sunshine State in 1968.

Florida's system of public education is, and always has been, the offspring of two controlling parents: politics (elections and governance) and industry (wealth and corporate profits). This marriage of convenience has lasted more than a century; but these particular parents didn't stay married all those years for the sake of the children. They stayed married to protect their own vested interests: power, profit, and low taxes.

Florida's political rulers and business moguls have always scratched each other's backs to facilitate getting elected and/or making money, and the lynchpin for their success has been keeping the state's taxes low. Their low tax philosophy is, of course, shared by many of Florida's citizens, but those citizens look to their political and business leaders to set priorities appropriately as they fulfill their constitutional obligations.

This book is the story of a colossal conflict in 1968 between Florida's government and the state's teachers who were represented by the Florida Education Association. That conflict pitted the economic and political priorities of the business community, the governor and the legislature against the educational concerns of the state's teachers. The confrontation didn't spring up overnight; it had been smoldering for decades.

The altercation in Florida burst onto the nation's radar screen forty years ago when decaying conditions in the education system had reached the point where 35,000 Florida teachers felt they had to resign their positions in order to stem the decay. They had waited and waited, year after year, for someone—anyone—to reform an education system that had atrophied to the point of scandal. They had lobbied, implored, demanded, threatened, and warned—all to no avail.

Finally, when no one else would step up to the plate, the state's teachers came to believe they had no other option than to leave their classrooms in protest. When they did so, they came face to face with an entrenched power structure that was willing to run roughshod over the lives and careers of its educators in order to maintain a chronically sick, status quo tax system. Why was that the case? Why wouldn't the legislature, the governor, and the state's business interests come up with enough money to improve an admittedly bad situation?

The answer, no matter how it was gussied up or rationalized, is that Florida's legislature, governor, and business community were unwilling to raise taxes. Forty years ago, these Florida power brokers, in league with most local school boards, proudly wore the economic straightjackets they had carefully stitched together for themselves over several generations. Their low tax mindset had become an institutional obsession that, like a swarm of army ants, overpowered anything in its path.

Florida had (and still has) a constitutional prohibition against a state income tax. It was (and is) a state with low property taxes compared to other states. Its citizens and their elected representatives were (and still are) more than happy to rely on tourists to pay for as many of Florida's needs as possible through sales taxes.

Before proceeding to tell this disturbing but inspiring story, a few of the author's biases and use of terminology are in order.

First, this book is not an academic study of the teacher walkout. It is an account of what happened and why written as honestly and accurately as possible. It is, however, told largely from the point of view of the courageous educators who almost a half-century ago put their jobs and careers on the line for the children they taught.

The author was present in Florida for three weeks during the walkout in 1968 and witnessed firsthand many of the events captured in the telling of this story. It should also be acknowledged that he is not an independent and impartial observer, having been a lifelong teacher advocate with a thirty-eight-year professional career of dedication to teachers and their organizations. He also served as the executive director of NEA's reconstituted Florida state affiliate, FTP–NEA, for three years in the late 1970s.

Having said that, no apology is offered for the perspective from which this book is written. The views of the striking teachers were never conveyed successfully during the education crisis of 1968. In fact, those who participated in the strike were relentlessly excoriated in scathing editorials and op-ed pieces from most of Florida's newspapers. They were vilified publicly by much of the business community, and local citizens all too often maligned them personally within their own communities.

Back then, no matter how hard teachers attempted to explain the reasons for their actions, and no matter how eloquently or graphically they described the awful state of public education in Florida, their exhortations fell on deaf ears. In short, their side of the story has been long overdue. Perhaps with the advantage of hindsight, coupled with the healing balm of time, the story can be appreciated in a more understanding and empathetic light.

The term "teachers" is used throughout the book when referring to those who walked out, but many of those who left their jobs were school administrators: building principals, central office personnel, and the like. In some ways the courage exemplified by those administrators surpassed even that of their teaching colleagues because the administrators knew full well that they were significantly more vulnerable than their teaching colleagues to losing their jobs or being otherwise punished for their action.

The Florida Education Association commissioned the writing of this book in early 2008 as part of the commemoration of the walkout's fortieth anniversary. While FEA commissioned the book, it imposed no constrictions, directions, or limitations on the author. He was provided an unfettered hand to do the research and write the story. The only admonition received from FEA was to tell the truth.

FEA always referred to the teachers' action as a "walkout," refusing to call it a strike. This was true because in addition to the membership's squeamishness over the word *strike*, FEA took the ill-advised legal position that if the teachers *resigned*, a case could arguably be made that the action was not a strike at all (strikes by public employees were and still are illegal in the State of Florida). Although walkout was the term used by FEA at the time, few in the news media or in the legislature used that terminology; most called it a strike. For purposes of this book, the author uses the terms walkout and strike interchangeably because to him it is a distinction without a difference.

Regardless of what it was called, the 1968 event constituted a statewide refusal of 35,000 Florida educators to continue working in an atrophying educational environment. What those teachers did in Florida forty years ago took more than courage. It took an overwhelming dedication to their profession and profound empathy with their students.

During the 1968 crisis, the author witnessed things that he will never forget. The fortitude that it took for teachers to leave their classrooms en masse for something they believed in, and then remain out in the face of the tremendous pressures placed upon them amazed many people. It still does four decades later.

At the time of the strike neither Florida's power structure nor its citizens appreciated the sacrifices teachers made or even why they made them. Neither did they understand the cause of the strike in the first place. The vast majority of observers simply assumed that it was a fight over teachers' salaries or money. That assumption prevails to this day. Nevertheless, the citizens of Florida, whether they know it or not, whether they appreciate it or not, or whether they even care or not, owe a tremendous debt of gratitude to their teachers—past and present. This book is about those teachers and that debt.

ACKNOWLEDGMENTS

Writing a book is never easy, but it can go along fairly smoothly if the author can rely on friends, colleagues, and other writers to help. Such is the case with this effort. The Florida Education Association (FEA) and its president, Andy Ford, deserve the lion's share of the credit for having the foresight to commemorate the contribution made by those FEA members who, forty years ago, put it all on the line for education in Florida. Andy's decision to make 2008 the fortieth anniversary celebration year of the 1968 walkout is both appropriate and deserving.

Special thanks must go to Jim Geiger, 1968 walkout veteran and former FEA officer and staff member, who conceived the recognition program and advocated for it. He was also a good friend, advisor, and critic during the writing of this book.

Another person who merits special mention is Bob Lee, who has been a stalwart officer, staffer, and activist in FEA for decades and a friend of mine over the years regardless of which side of the organizational fence we each worked. Bob has also been a strong advocate for recognition of the teachers who walked off their jobs in 1968. His advice and counsel is greatly appreciated.

Finally, Tom Fackender, current and longtime FEA staff member, was invaluable to me as a mentor, editor, and researcher in the writing of this book. We share a love of organizational history and baseball.

Aaron Wallace, former FEA chief of staff, and Jeff Wright, FEA director of public policy advocacy, also provided much appreciated support and encouragement.

In addition, although I will not list all those who were interviewed or provided assistance, the following people were especially helpful:

- Braulio Alonzo (former NEA president, former Hillsborough principal and strike veteran)
- Beverly Barberi, (former Escambia teacher and strike veteran)
- Richard Batchelder, former NEA president, former executive director of FEA and FEA/United
- Ruth Cameron (spouse, Escambia strike veteran, former FTP–NEA president)
- Howard Carroll (former NEA PR staff member and 1968 NEA strike staff)
- Bob Chanin (NEA general counsel)
- Phil Constans (former FEA executive secretary)
- Rod Davis (Pasco strike veteran and former FEA board member)
- Barbara DeVane (former Suwannee teacher, leader, and strike veteran)
- Bea Griswold, (former Pinellas teacher, leader, and strike veteran)
- Terry Herndon (former NEA executive director)
- Gail Husbands (Escambia teacher, current Escambia E.A. president),
- Tom Koerner (publisher, Rowman & Littlefield)
- Dorothy Massie (former NEA staffer and editor of 1966 NEA PR&R Report)
- Ken Melley (former NEA staffer and book advisor)
- Swinson Schipman (former Escambia teacher and strike veteran)
- Larry Sorensen, (former NEA staff member and 1968 NEA strike staff)
- Mary Stanley (former Escambia teacher and strike veteran)
- Jim Williams (former NEA staffer and 1968 NEA strike staff)

Finally, grateful recognition must go to every one of the 35,000 teachers and administrators who participated in the 1968 walkout. Their effort was courageous, their mission noble, and their legacy eternal.

1

GOOD SCHOOLS, LOW TAXES

Since 1513, when Ponce de Leon slogged through the peninsula's swamps in search of an elusive Fountain of Youth, the state's ambiance has beckoned those seeking a toastier life. For over a century, flocks of snowbirds abandoned their frigid nests in the north to migrate south to Florida. After World War II, émigrés from other states scrambled to Florida by the hundreds of thousands to bask in the state's bountiful sunshine.

However, legions of migrants headed to Florida for an altogether different reason: to escape the higher taxes they had been paying back in their home states. These Middle Americans, many of them retirees on fixed incomes, were lured south by Florida's well-deserved reputation as a low tax state. They could buy a house in Florida comparable to the one they left up north and cut their property taxes by half, or maybe three-quarters. Also, Florida's constitutional prohibition against any state income tax was an inducement that caused untold numbers of families to pack up the dog and kids and head to Florida. What these families were searching for in the Sunshine State wasn't a geriatric Fountain of Youth, but an economic one.

There were plenty of other reasons why voyagers were drawn to the Sunshine State. Job seekers sought employment in the developing real estate, citrus, cattle, transportation, space, and tourist industries. Many families came to Florida because of its plethora of military bases and wide variety of related cottage industries. After President Harry Truman established Cape Canaveral on Florida's east central coast in 1949, the space program added its luster to the state's magnetic appeal. Less motivated newcomers sought to enjoy life on a palm-tree-lined golf course or just chill out on a hot beach.

Accessibility to venture capital attracted entrepreneurs to Florida on a wide variety of fronts: real estate, condominium development, beachfront properties, insurance, recreational facilities, strip malls, amusement parks, and so forth. One of the primary reasons business people relocated to Florida was to take advantage of the munificent tax breaks the state bestowed on business and industry. Florida's economy grew as industries became more and more robust, business boomed, and millionaires proliferated.

Times were good in the Sunshine State.

Prior to World War II, less than two million people lived in Florida, but by the time of the teacher walkout in 1968 the population was pushing six million. In the three decades following the war, baby boomers joined the influx of migrants causing Florida's population literally to explode (see table 1.1).[1]

Table 1.1.

Decade	Net Population Growth
• 1940 to 1950	873,000
• 1950 to 1960	2,180,000
• 1960 to 1970	1,839,000

Fully three-quarters of this astounding growth in the 1950s and 1960s was due to migration from other states, causing Florida to lag behind only California in that regard.[2] The rush of people to Florida meant that the state's government needed to provide every new resident with public services such as police and fire protection, health care, and education. Of course, providing services required the state to raise sufficient tax revenue to get the job done.

And, that is exactly where the rub begins. There have always been two elements in Florida's economic culture that were anathema to providing enough revenue for public services: myopic government stewardship of public funds, and a historic bias against adequate taxation. Those characteristics can easily be traced back to Florida's original 1868 constitution that deliberately set up a system of weak state government, local autonomy, incentives for the accumulation of individual wealth, land interests, and low taxation.[3] Through the years, those elements have survived as the state's most cherished values, and the vigilant sentinels who guard them are an amalgam of rural interests, wealthy landowners, profit-driven industrialists, and big business entrepreneurs.

For over a century the state's legislature and cabinet operated primarily through informal backroom deals ordered up by powerful lobbyists. Consequently, Florida's legislature and cabinet became part and parcel of the very interests they were supposed to be regulating, and the elected government became little more than a shadow government for private interests.

The state became shrouded in a corrupt miasma of accumulated wealth for individuals and businesses, and in the process turned its back on public services. Issues related to environmental protection, adequate infrastructures, sensible zoning laws, and quality education went begging. It got so bad that although the various state agencies met in public session, they were merely ratifying decisions that had already been made behind closed doors.[4] The philosophy of those wielding power could well have been described as, "We take care of each other and to hell with the common good."

Their refusal to pay attention to public service was unfortunate because Florida's expanding population needed an infrastructure that would accommodate its increasingly large footprint. The state required more housing, water, roads, electricity, school buildings, police and fire protection, and the like. The power structure viewed the constant pressure to meet infrastructure needs and expand public services as not only a nuisance, but also a serious threat to the economic status quo.

That power structure held domain over Florida's legislature and cabinet for many generations, and its most sacred mission was to keep taxes in an anorexic state. Good politics went hand in hand with good profits, and good profits, in turn, went hand in hand with low taxes. In order to keep taxes low, Florida's power structure willfully allowed public services, especially education, to atrophy.

Arguably the most pressing public policy issue the state had to face in the two decades after World War II was providing a quality education for the burgeoning number of children banging on its schoolhouse doors. In the single decade prior to 1968, the year of the statewide teachers' strike, the population in the public schools had swollen by more than 50 percent,[5] creating a prodigious need for additional school resources, that is, funds.

The rising tide of students brought with it a proportional rise in the cost of educating them. Florida's education system needed more buildings, more books, more teachers, more kindergartens, better curricula, more and better special education programs; in short, the system required more of virtually everything. Normally when states face such a challenge, it is natural and appropriate for them to look to their citizens to share the financial burden by paying requisite taxes. Axiomatically, the more citizens there are demanding services, the more citizens there are to pay the bill. That is, after all, the whole idea of taxation: to finance the services needed for the public good. It is the very essence of America's system of government.

Calculating the formula relating to services versus taxes doesn't involve quantum physics or metaphysical contemplation. Simply stated, when a state increases its taxes sufficiently to fund its public schools, the supply (money) meets the demand (more kids in school needing a quality education). In American society, providing a quality education for students is based on, and governed by, this rather basic and uncomplicated idea.

However, when a state like Florida *fails* to increase its taxes commensurate with the legitimate needs of public education, the process is reversed: the supply fails to meet the demand. In Florida, because the primary determination has always been to keep taxes low, educational needs became tertiary at best.

During the 1960s, successive legislative sessions refused to raise taxes in the face of dramatically increased educational costs and grievously underfunded the state's education budgets. By refusing to raise taxes, the state flipped the supply-demand formula upside down, leaving Florida's children and teachers as helpless as a turtle on its back. During the period 1963 to 1967, the years immediately preceding the teacher walkout, the cost of education escalated significantly, but the Florida legislature's education appropriations actually declined from 54.6 percent to 53.7 percent.[6]

Education funding in Florida had slipped severely out of whack, and the state's willingness to sacrifice quality public education on the altar of tax suppression cheated both students and teachers of the resources they needed. While that strategy served the short-term objectives of the state's politicians (immediate political gratification), it did precious little to fulfill the legislatures' obligations to education as defined in the state constitution.

Right up to the time of the teacher walkout in 1968, the feudal barons of Florida were still ignoring the rising costs of public education. These feudal barons were largely legislators from the northern and central part of the state. They were dubbed "The Porkchop Gang," and had become the dominant element in the Florida power structure. They received their Porkchop Gang appellation from an editorial in the *Tampa Tribune* that claimed they were "fighting for pork rather than principle."[7]

By the middle 1960s, the one-two punch of consistent education underfunding and chronically low taxes had teachers on the ropes. Their legs already wobbly, the legislature and governor pummeled them even more by demanding that they do more and more with less and less. Florida's legislators remained perfectly content to scrape along with a cut-rate, bargain basement educational system. Unfortunately, things had gone far beyond simply trying to maintain bargain basement quality. Florida's power structure had created an educational sinkhole.

As education program improvements were rejected year after year, so were increases in teachers' pay. In 1965, for example, with teachers' salaries already a huge problem, a legislative committee killed a proposed $51 million teacher pay raise, forcing teachers to continue subsidizing the state's truancy. As the state's education budget became increasingly depressed, so did the teachers' morale. The sinkhole was widening and Florida teachers were sliding into the abyss.

Politicians would occasionally try to finesse mounting teacher frustration by promising improvements, but those promises were invariably exposed as nothing more than transparent political posturing. Like the story of the boy who cried wolf, the state's teachers had stopped responding to the phony laments and crocodile tears of low tax politicians.

When it came to posturing, Florida's politicians were in a class by themselves, and they saved their most disingenuous behavior for the campaign trail. It was while on the stump that they performed routines worthy of vaudeville headliners. First they would sing the praises of teachers, then they'd strike heroic poses and emote about their commitment to a quality education for every Florida child (you could almost hear "school days" being hummed in the background). They would gnash their teeth while remonstrating against low teacher salaries.

The personification of this act appeared on stage during the 1966 gubernatorial campaign. Candidate Claude Kirk Jr., a real scenery chewer if there ever was one, promised voters that he would "make Florida education the best in America while allowing no increase in taxes." As ridiculous as that pledge was on its face, a majority of Floridians bought it.

The more the state's education system deteriorated, the more the hypocrisy of the state's double standard became palpable. Florida demanded that teachers provide quality instruction to their students no matter what, but thought nothing of abrogating its own obligations to those students. In the mid 1960s, after years of educational neglect, teacher depression morphed into frustration, and then frustration turned into anger. The angrier the teachers became, the more they agitated for their professional organization, the Florida Education Association, to do something about the situation. They wanted action.

By 1968 the gap between the demands placed on education by the ever-expanding population and the state's anemic tax revenues had widened the sinkhole to the size of a chasm. No matter how bad the education crisis became, however, additional funding for education remained out of the question—especially when Claude Kirk Jr. was elected Florida's thirty-sixth governor in 1966.

As governor, Kirk was more than willing to shuttle existing educational funds from one underfunded place in the budget to another underfunded place in the budget, but he would not tolerate any improvements that required a tax increase. The education crisis was reaching its crescendo as Florida's real estate agents continued to sell houses to prospective buyers with the ludicrous but appealing enticement: "Good schools, low taxes."

The self-delusion was about to end.

2

LOW TAX OBSESSION

There is nothing really shocking about Florida being a low tax–low service state; it always has been, and it still is. It is no secret that even today the low tax weeds still bloom in Florida's political garden. The endemic culture of suppressing taxes at the expense of public services was chiseled into Florida's escutcheon right from the beginning by the forbearers of the infamous Porkchop Gang. Their institutionalized principles paid off handsomely for the private sector and politicians, but they have been nothing short of catastrophic for Florida public services generally and education in particular.

Those who originally wielded the chisels were men of means who carved and shaped Florida's political and economic systems to serve their own interests. They were land barons, railroad tycoons, citrus magnets, well-heeled farmers, prosperous industrialists, and opportunistic politicians. They did their chiseling well, because over the years the credo of downplaying public service while lionizing individual and corporate wealth was commonly accepted in government antechambers, corporate boardrooms, grange halls, and even churches. It had become an integral part of Florida's government and culture, as comfortable as an old blanket.

In Florida's earlier days, when the state was largely agrarian and sparsely populated, the Porkchop pioneers helped themselves to a tropical paradise of spring-fed rivers, lush vegetation, keys, mangrove swamps, manatees, alligators, white sand beaches, dolphins, sharks, live oaks, Spanish moss, canopy roads, palm trees, coconuts, and massive infusions of sunshine.

As a result of the state's institutional mindset to keep taxes low, Florida's taxes became, indeed, substantially lower than those of most other states throughout the country. Florida is one of only six states with no state income tax whatsoever, the others being Alaska, Nevada, South Dakota, Texas, and Wyoming.[1] In the other forty-four states, state income taxes range from one percent to over seven percent of their residents' earnings.[2]

Florida has always relied heavily on sales taxes to take up some of the slack, but twenty other states have equal or higher sales tax rates than Florida.[3] To add to the problem, the taxes Florida levied on business and industry ranged from very low to virtually nothing, especially through the 1960s. The bottom line is that when Florida's low tax status is combined with the relatively healthy income of its citizens (Florida's per capita income is high), Florida could have—and should have—done much, much better with its education funding.

As a result of Florida's historic low tax obsession, by the time of the teachers' strike in 1968, the state's citizens had been conditioned to expect low taxes regardless of public need. Particularly regarding education, they had come to expect something for nothing, or at least something for very little. The low tax obsession held sway over the state even as Florida underwent a transformational change from rural to urban and from population sparsity to density, particularly in the southern part of the state. Even with these population shifts, the old, rural power structure continued to reign supreme.

The role of the business community in suppressing public service funding in Florida should not be overlooked. From the outset, Florida's industrial and corporate interests became fierce promoters of low taxes and minimalist government. To them less government oversight meant more corporate autonomy, and more corporate autonomy meant more profit.

It was precisely government's inattention and lack of oversight that led to the catastrophic destruction of Florida's ecology by industrial forces. For many years, Florida industries unabashedly polluted the water and destroyed the land to the point where the state's ecology and quality of life were literally in peril. It wasn't until the 1960s that wildlife groups and reformers, with the help of Governor LeRoy Collins, finally stopped them. It's a sad but true fact that Florida's industries didn't care any more about education than it did about the ecology.

Other businesses, especially banks, brokerage houses, lending institutions, and insurance companies, wholeheartedly joined the ranks of those fighting against taxation and government oversight. As a result, the state's incentives for businesses were abundant: minimal government regulation, nonexistent zoning requirements, few environmental restrictions, and, most alluring of all, very low taxes on everybody and everything.

Wealthy landholders also anted up to feed the low tax obsession. Many of them were patrons of long-held tracts of Florida land who paid fewer taxes per acre on their property than more recent, smaller landowners. One thing was certain. In Florida those who had the money and power called the shots and exerted enormous influence over Florida government.

Edward Ball, an industrialist who controlled the vast Dupont interests in railroads, banking, and woodpulp, was arguably the most powerful figure in Florida and, although atypical in many respects, a perfect symbol of the parsimonious thinking that dominated the state's power brokers.[4] Ball held great influence with the Pork Chop Gang, and his impact on government and public policy during the first half of the twentieth century was staggering. He was fiercely antilabor and notoriously frugal even as he ran the entire DuPont enterprise.

The rural domination of the Florida legislature existed for a century or more because the legislature was never apportioned on a one person–one vote basis. Incredibly, the rural counties in the northern and central parts of the state had as many or more representatives than the more populated areas. It wasn't until 1967, when the U.S. Supreme Court ruled that the way Florida apportioned itself was unconstitutional, that reapportionment of Florida's House and Senate districts finally took place. Only then did the previously malapportioned legislature begin to reflect more accurately the state's population centers, and only then did the rural interests begin to cede total control.

Another jolt to the Good Old Boy's domination of Florida's governance apparatus occurred when a new state constitution was adopted in 1968. Nevertheless, even as these new mandates caused the scenery on stage to change somewhat, the low tax puppeteers continued to pull the legislature's strings from behind the curtain.

Given a century or more to gain a solid foothold, the low tax culture in Florida had became like a powerful narcotic that dulled the state's social senses. It had become an obsession that all but obliterated the state's political courage.

3

CLAUDIUS MAXIMUS

Without question, the 1960s were unsettled and turbulent times. It was a decade of rebellion, renaissance, violence, and hope. Looming over everything else was the immensely unpopular war raging in Vietnam, a war that shanghaied almost 600,000 young Americans to fight in Far East jungles and sent millions of Americans to the streets in protest.

Across the United States, riots engulfed many American cities as African Americans struggled to achieve equal rights. The struggle for school desegregation was in full swing during the 1960s (Florida's schools remained segregated for more than fifteen years after the 1954 *Brown v. Board of Education* Supreme Court decision). In April 1968, just two short months after the Florida statewide teacher walkout, Dr. Martin Luther King Jr. was assassinated while championing workers' rights in Memphis, Tennessee. Two short months after that, Senator Robert Kennedy was assassinated in Los Angeles while campaigning for president.

Unrest during the 1960s also swirled around the most recent iteration of the women's movement in America. After two hundred years of discrimination against women, many people placed their hopes for female equality in the contentious battle for passage of the Equal Rights Amendment. Both national teacher organizations—the National Education Association (NEA) and the American Federation of Teachers (AFT)—were deeply committed to that effort, as was the Florida Education Association.

On top of all this, teachers across the nation were standing up for themselves, rejecting a century or more of patronization and neglect. Teacher organizations like the Florida Education Association (FEA) were becoming more militant because its members had become increasingly disillusioned with the empty blandishments of professionalism that were being served up by the establishment in lieu of bread and butter.

Across the country, even in states that had no collective bargaining laws for teachers, virtually every state had shown at least some initiative in securing necessary resources (including tax increases) to fund public education and address the issue of low teacher salaries. Not in Florida, however, where the public schools were in the throes of an education depression brought on by generations of financial neglect. As public education deteriorated year after year, teachers approached the brink of desperation; they needed something or someone to give them hope.

The hope they craved didn't flicker for even a nanosecond when Claude Kirk Jr., dubbed "Claudius Maximus" by the Miami *Herald*, was elected governor in 1966. He was the first Republican governor elected in Florida since Reconstruction and swaggered into the governor's mansion after defeating Democrat Miami mayor Robert King High. High had gained the Democrat nomination after beating the incumbent governor Haydon Burns in a divisive and bruising Democrat primary.

During the general election, Kirk relentlessly attacked High from one end of the state to the other, accusing him of being a liberal who was unable to control crime in Miami. In his campaign, Kirk promised to fight corruption and champion education. He railed against the Democrats' control of the legislature and professed great disdain for Florida's cabinet system. Who was this Republican upstart and how did he fare as governor? More importantly, what was his role in the statewide teacher strike?

Kirk was a bigger than life character, one of those rare people who comes along every generation or so and can't be pigeonholed or reduced to a common denominator. Florida's new governor was a political one-man gang, a composite of Huey Long, Douglas McArthur, and P. T. Barnum. Kirk was flamboyant, confrontational, egocentric, ambitious, vindictive, wealthy, and totally unpredictable. He not only took pride in confronting anyone who disagreed with him, but he took no prisoners. Probably his most dominant characteristic, however, was a penchant for publicity, even if it was negative.

Claude Roy Kirk Jr. was born in San Bernadino, California, in 1926, and was a Marine veteran of World War II and Korea. He earned a B.S. degree from Emory University in 1945 and a law degree from the University of Alabama in 1949. When he moved to Jacksonville, Florida, in 1956 he became president of the American Heritage Life Insurance Company, an institution he grew into a highly successful enterprise largely through his consummate skills as a salesman and glad-hander. He ran unsuccessfully for the U.S. Senate in 1964 as a Republican after having previously been a Democrat.

Kirk liked to boast that he enjoyed nothing more than a good fight, although many of his contemporaries claimed that he loved being in the limelight even more. In Kirk's mind, the best of all worlds was to pick a fight in public with the media hanging on his every word. He was not a consensus builder by any definition, but was just the opposite: a political bully determined to get his way regardless of who or what stood in his path. His chief of staff, Wade Hopping put it this way: "He would beat you up or bust your chops."[1] Kirk called it leadership, but others called it intimidation.

Kirk's addiction to drama and his penchant for confrontation made him immensely controversial—and temporarily successful. While his un-orthodox approach worked with the public in the short term, it didn't take long before people concluded that publicity motivated their new governor more than issues. Like most egocentric personalities, Governor Kirk craved more than publicity; he craved notoriety and was constantly in search of a higher, more visible, mountain to climb.

Although politically conservative in most areas, Kirk's fellow conser-vatives were not inoculated from his attacks. He tromped on many Repub-lican members of the legislature, and frequently strayed from traditional Republican writ. His administration was a wild ride for the State of Florida: controversial, rowdy, stormy, and sometimes undignified, but it was never dull. He was an equal opportunity despot who fought with Repub-licans, Democrats, and Independents—and loved every minute of it.

Governor Kirk was not without his good points. He had big ideas and to some degree was a visionary. His reputation for loving children was well deserved. He hated Florida's history of corruptive influences within the legislature and cabinet. He despised organized crime and worked closely with police agencies to eradicate it.

Kirk's problem with government and governing was his self-centered and self-serving approach to leadership. He was not tolerant of those who wouldn't subordinate themselves to him and his causes. In his mind, the task of the leader was to determine the course, proclaim it, and then move for-ward. The job of subordinates was to shut up and follow orders.[2] Governor Kirk played only one game—his, and played by one set of rules—his own.

Kirk maintained publicly that if you aren't controversial, no one knows you're alive. When the opportunity came along for a full-throated, public confrontation with the state's educators and FEA, their "union," Kirk saw an opportunity for everyone to see just how alive he was. In all likelihood, the prospect of a public shoot-out with Florida's teachers made the governor salivate like one of Pavlov's dogs. In a speech at the National Governor's Conference in 1967, Kirk boasted, "This is Claude Kirk. Do you read my press? Then you know I'm a tree-shakin' son of a bitch."[3] On more than one occasion he told reporters that he intended to break the teachers' back.

Instead of trying to break their back, Claude Kirk could have provided the leadership that teachers craved by becoming the education hero that he promised to be during his campaign. That kind of leadership wasn't in the cards, however, because it was neither in his nature nor on his agenda. First of all, Kirk didn't share the teachers' angst about the disastrous condition of public schools or public education.

His vision of, and dedication to, education reform involved getting more efficiency from the tax dollars already appropriated and bringing technology to the classroom. He was interested in the computer age and saw the potential for computers in the classroom before most others did. As far as teachers were concerned, they had no quarrel with the governor's desire to bring technology to the classroom, but they considered it akin to offering an umbrella to someone standing in a hurricane. They needed textbooks, erasers, chalk, smaller classes, more desks, and repairs to leaky roofs and cracked windows before they could take advantage of technology.

In a typical political display designed to give the illusion of progress, the new governor sponsored no less than four statewide education conferences during the first four months of his tenure, none of which accomplished anything more than kicking the can down the road. As far as the governor was concerned, inadequate school buildings, the acute need for textbooks and equipment, the lack of special education and kindergarten programs, or the near slave-wages teachers received were all issues he could only solve without raising taxes.

Instead, the governor was focused on a range of noneducation issues that he considered a higher priority; that is to say, issues he could accomplish without raising taxes. For example, Kirk had long fulminated against Florida's cabinet system, which he considered corrupt (with justification). He publicly referred to his own cabinet as "The Seven Dwarfs" and criticized them to the media. He called them stupid, especially Commissioner of Education Floyd Christian.

Kirk wanted to reorganize the cabinet system and put Christian out of his elected post, making it an appointed position. Floyd Christian had previously been superintendent of schools in Pinellas County before accepting the post at the state level. When describing Christian, a former football player and coach in Pinellas, Kirk took frequent delight in saying, "Floyd Christian could do everything with a football but sign it."[4] During the 1968 teacher walkout, Christian, who had expressed support for FEA, tried to be a mediating force, offering several plans for compromise. Kirk, however, opposed everything Christian stood for, especially if it meant compromising with FEA.

Another reason Kirk had little time for teachers' concerns was that he had political and personal fish to fry. His political ambitions were national in scope, and right after being elected governor, he launched an effort to inject himself into the 1968 presidential campaign as a vice-presidential running mate. Kirk ham-handedly finagled with Richard Nixon during the Republican primaries to be on his ticket, but to no avail. (Nixon ultimately chose Spiro Agnew of Maryland as his vice presidential selection.) Kirk then maneuvered, also unsuccessfully, to get Nelson Rockefeller to anoint him as his running mate. (Rockefeller, of course, never got the nomination.)

Kirk's personal life was also a priority. After his election, the governor married a beautiful blonde, Erika Mattfeld, who he had been dating and teasingly christened Madame X to the media during his campaign. He and his new bride were often out of the state living the grand life with Florida taxpayers often footing the bill. Kirk frequently sailed his 37-foot sloop off the coast of southern Florida and averaged about 10,000 miles a month flying out of state in his private Lear jet. He once referred to his frequent absences from Florida as part of "the Kirk plan for instant controversy."[5]

His high living, which at first seemed charmingly eccentric to many, soon appeared less benign. When challenged by a reporter at a news conference about the state paying for a large part of Kirk's honeymoon, the governor looked the reporter straight in the eyes and said, "I'm delighted . . . suppose you never found that out and a political enemy found it later?" He then offered the reporter a reward for digging up the facts.[6]

But, the most important reason why the governor could not provide Florida's teachers with any hope for a better education system was that, despite all his reformist rhetoric and populist pronouncements, Kirk was a loyal soldier in Florida's low tax army. He was a rock-ribbed, inflexible, uncompromising, intransigent supporter of Florida's low tax obsession.

As indicated earlier, Kirk had run for governor on the absurd but appealing conceit of promising "no increased taxes" while making Florida "first in the nation in education." Kirk's bogus campaign pledge was music to the ears of the antitax crowd, but ominous and foreboding to the state's teachers. They feared that the bad times they had been experiencing for years were about to get much worse, and they were right.

In no time flat after being elected, it became obvious to the governor that he could not improve education without raising taxes; so instead, he killed education improvement and dumped the body overboard without so much as a farewell salute to the corpse. Kirk routinely vetoed bills approved by the Democrat majority in the legislature, and the Republican minority, mostly out of loyalty to party unity, supported the governor's vetoes even when they disagreed with him.

Having said that, Republican legislators received little reciprocity. They found that out in spades in 1970 when Kirk stabbed them in the back over the issue of legislative pay raises. The story is illustrative. Since way back in 1885 the state had limited legislators' pay to $1,200 per year, and the 1969 legislature wanted to increase that pay to $12,000. The legislature, Democrats and Republicans alike, passed the bill only to have Kirk veto it.

What bothered the Republicans most about the veto was that they would never have allowed the bill to be brought to the floor for a vote in the first place if they had known that Kirk's veto was in the offing. Their minority leader, Don Reed of Palm Beach, had assured everyone that he had received a green light from the governor indicating that he was on board with the raise.

Reed always maintained, in fact, that in offering his support for the bill, Kirk even admonished him that $12,000 wasn't enough. All during the lead-up to the bill's passage, Kirk said nothing about the raise publicly. Nor did he object when the pay raise bill passed.[7] However, after several newspapers around the state began to raise hell about the pay increases, Kirk, without missing a beat, threw his Republican colleagues under the bus, claiming that he was never consulted and never gave his approval to the deal.

Not only did he veto the bill, he called a joint session of the legislature so he could publicly reprimand the legislators to their faces, including his Republican allies. Then he threw fuel onto the fire by attacking Reed personally. Kirk, with his eye on reelection in 1970, played to the media and the public at the expense of his loyal Republican colleagues. The legislature, furious and frustrated, overrode Kirk's veto, but it was the last straw for many Republicans.

When Kirk ran for reelection in 1970 as an incumbent against Democrat Reubin Askew, he received only 43 percent of the popular vote. Askew, a state senator from Pensacola, was universally recognized as a decent, dedicated, moderate politician. During the 1970 campaign, Kirk called Askew "a nice, sweet-looking fellow, but being governor is a tough job and being a mamma's boy won't get the job done."[8]

Few Republican legislators supported Kirk in the 1970 election; in fact, many worked for Askew behind the scenes. Kirk met his ignominious political end with practically no one in either party shedding a tear. They didn't even get misty-eyed. As a footnote, eight years later in 1978, in true Kirksonian fashion, he pushed back the lid on his political coffin, swooshed his tattered black cape across his face, and ran for governor *as a Democrat.*

Governor Kirk was not the sole cause of FEA's statewide strike by any means. Other governors and other legislatures had brought the state to the point of crisis, and the antitax culture had more than abetted them. He was, however, the strike's catalyst. When he became governor, Florida's education system was already on life support, but Kirk stepped on its feeding tube. Because teachers were experiencing frustration beyond measure, his antics only exacerbated the situation.

The added negative dimension that Kirk provided, and the thing that set him apart from previous governors, was his boastful, confrontational behavior. He also brought to bear a swaggering insensitivity that was more than enough to push the teachers over the edge. After decades of insufficient rain, the educational underbrush had become dry as tinder. The legislature poured gasoline on it, and Kirk showed up with a lighted match.

By the time he left office after a single term, Claude Kirk Jr. had confronted numerous individuals and institutions, including his own legislature and cabinet. His confrontation with FEA, however, was arguably the biggest of all; it certainly had the most repercussions.

The real tragedy for Governor Kirk and the State of Florida was that he could not only have avoided the strike if he had chosen to do so, but he could have been the hero that education and educators in Florida desperately needed. It's rather sad that Claude Kirk Jr., for all his charisma, bluster, and style, left office seen largely as a political buffoon.

4

DOOMSDAY MACHINE

Long before the statewide teachers strike, Florida's low tax beast had wrapped its arms around the state's body politic, squeezing until there was little breath left. By the time the 1960s arrived, the situation for education was grim. Three consecutive "hold the line" legislative sessions in the early 1960s were followed by the 1965 legislative session that provided no pay raise for teachers and virtually no funding increase for K–12 public schools. It scuttled each and every proposal for a tax increase; then told teachers to get money from their counties.[1]

The callousness of the 1965 legislature toward education was symptomatic of the dismissive attitude of the power structure in responding to FEA's entreaties. At the conclusion of almost every unsuccessful session, the legislature threw the funding onus back to beleaguered local school districts. After the legislature would pass the buck to the counties, the counties often just passed the buck—period. They couldn't always be blamed, however, because no matter how desperately some of them pleaded with the local citizenry for more millage, they were often rejected.

The handoff to local districts was meaningless because local school districts would either refuse to seek additional funding or often fail when they tried. Particularly in the rural areas of Florida, counties were stocked with retirees from the Midwest and Northeast who lived on fixed incomes, and getting voters to approve increased property taxes was extremely difficult. Less than about 25 percent of local populations had children in school, and people often complained that they didn't see why they should have to support schools financially when they had no children in them.

Buck-passing and obfuscation between the legislature and local county school districts had become somewhat the norm. Because legislators chose not to raise taxes at the state level, and districts couldn't or wouldn't raise them locally, teachers were left holding only bones and feathers. With nowhere else to turn, they pushed both their local associations and the Florida Education Association (FEA) to become more aggressive.

One might legitimately ask just who *is* responsible for the appropriate funding of education in Florida? The answer to that question is not a mystery. The Florida Constitution places the responsibility for establishing and funding public schools squarely on the shoulders of the state legislature. Its mandate is neither fuzzy nor indirect.

> *Section 8, 1,* (a) "The education of the children is a fundamental value of the people of the State of Florida. It is, therefore, a paramount duty of the state to make adequate provision for the education of all children residing within its boarders. *Adequate provision shall be made by law for a uniform, efficient, safe, secure, and high quality system of free public schools that allows students to obtain a high quality education* and for the establishment, maintenance, and operation of institutions of higher learning and other public education programs that the needs of the people may require.[2] [Emphasis added]

By the late 1960s, the continued neglect of education by the state legislature had reached a flash point. The numbers of students in Florida's schools had dramatically increased, but the legislature had chosen to ignore them. It was no less than amazing that the legislature and several successive governors, with the exception of LeRoy Collins, deliberately chose negligence as a strategy for dealing with Florida's educational needs.

In the two decades from 1945 to 1965 alone, school enrollments had increased by more than 50 percent, an astounding growth rate experienced by no other state. Yet, during that same period, very few schools were built and not nearly enough teachers were added to the personnel roles.[3] In truth, virtually every aspect of the public school system had fallen into disrepair.

Against this backdrop, the Florida Education Association issued warning after warning about the consequences for children stemming from the lack of educational resources and school system improvements. In spite of those warnings, and in spite of what the state's own data revealed, those with the power to do something to alleviate the situation did nothing. Instead of responding positively to FEA's admonitions, the legislature, governor, and business lobby chose to hunker down, resisting any improvement that meant raising taxes. Predictably and inexorably, the state's already atrophying education system began to cave in brick-by-brick, book-by-book, student-by-student, and teacher-by-teacher.

Years of the legislature's abandonment of proper education financing had caused the state's sixty-seven county school districts to gasp for air. By 1968 school boards were cutting back on already bare bones programs, teachers were going without salary increases, the physical conditions of schools were dreadful, class sizes were burgeoning, and students had to do without basic tools and supplies.

Many counties were left with a crumbling education infrastructure. Ramshackle buildings in egregious disrepair were inhospitable places in which to teach and learn, but they peppered Florida's landscape. Some buildings had windows boarded over or covered with ribbons of masking tape to stifle the expansion of cracks in the glass. In many urban districts, graffiti was everywhere and disheveled school buildings stood like abandoned warehouses along railroad tracks. In some western Florida counties, schools still used outhouses and teachers often had to buy toilet paper.

In many school buildings every vacant space, including hallways, custodial facilities, and large closets, had been converted to teaching rooms. It was commonplace for classrooms to be as crowded as rush-hour buses, with forty-five or more students jammed into rooms designed for half as many. Portable classrooms were everywhere and students and teachers were packed into them like pickles in a jar. Shortages of desks and laboratory equipment were commonplace, and many teachers dug into their already shallow pockets to provide money for chalk, erasers, books, maps, and other basics for their students.

The condition of textbooks ran the gamut from pitiful to nonexistent, and students often had to use books that were so old they were no longer relevant. During the 1968 strike, a young female teacher attending one of the daily meetings in a central Florida county lamented to me, "My science textbooks say that America might actually go into space some day. The NASA Mercury Project started ten years ago, for Pete's sake; we've been in orbit for six years." Her frustration was particularly ironic because the Kennedy Space Center was only a stone's throw down the road from her school.

Some teachers were using textbooks that had been discarded by other school districts years earlier. Beverly Barberi, an Escambia County junior high school teacher during the strike, said, "There were so many names of previous students written on the first page of my students' books that there wasn't room to add another one." In many schools, books had to be bound with duct tape because they were falling apart, and many students weren't allowed to take books home for fear they would disintegrate. For some classes, students had no textbooks at all.

Teachers had put up with all of it. And how were they remunerated for having to make-do without needed resources? The state's gratitude certainly wasn't reflected in the abysmally low salaries it paid them, which even fell below other southern states. At the time of the 1968 walkout, Florida ranked in the bottom half of states in teacher pay: below Georgia, Alabama, and Virginia. The average teacher salary in the state was $6,600 a year, almost $660 below the national average, and it took Florida teachers six or seven years to reach the $6,600 level. Starting teachers made less than $5,000.[4]

It wasn't uncommon for higher paid teachers to be released so that those earning a lower salary could be hired. If experienced teachers from other states came to Florida to teach, they were given only partial credit on the salary schedule for their years of experience; in other words, a teacher with twelve years' experience in another state would be paid at the level of a teacher with four or five years experience in Florida. Many teachers, fed up with the situation, left the state for better paying jobs elsewhere, refusing to wear a "kick me" sign on their backs any longer.

There was no masking the fact that teachers' salaries in Florida were a real problem. In his 1964 campaign for governor, Haydon Burns, in a classic example of political misdirection, stated, "I am concerned with the salaries for our teachers. Many of our counties are finding it increasingly difficult to staff our schools. The over-all salary scales are so low that they are unattractive to qualified teachers."[5] To no one's surprise, Burns did absolutely nothing about his "concern" after getting elected.

Teachers enjoyed no fringe benefits like health insurance, dental insurance, vision care, or personal days off. They did have a modest pension program (which they paid into themselves), but were not part of the Social Security system. They had twenty minute lunch periods during which they grabbed a bite while monitoring their students' behavior. In addition, they were frequently mandated to attend functions after school and on weekends with no additional pay. There were, of course, no collective bargaining agreements between local associations and school boards because there was no collective bargaining statute in the state.

Not to be overlooked in the school crisis forty years ago was the unremitting teacher shortage. Florida had an awful time recruiting and retaining teachers. Low pay and large class sizes discouraged many new teachers from accepting jobs in Florida. As a result, Florida had to find over 6,000 new teachers every year. FEA reported that Florida colleges and universities graduated almost 2,000 teachers a year, but only about half of them accepted teaching positions in the state. That meant that Florida had to recruit over 5,000 teachers every year from out of state—a prodigious task.

In refusing to do something about deteriorating school conditions, successive legislatures and governors routinely contended that there wasn't enough money to go around. While that rationalization was true insofar as it went, it blithely sidestepped the obvious option of getting more money. During the 1960s, legislatures chose to deal with increasing school costs by squeezing more and more from less and less. Teachers felt like they were forced to run faster and faster in a giant hamster wheel.

The lack of money pretext became more and more maddening to teachers because they knew full well that the legislature had no intention of ever raising taxes sufficient to improve the sorry state of education in Florida. The 1965 legislature, for example, appropriated an 11 percent increase in public school funding even though it knew full well that every penny of that money was required just to maintain the already appalling status quo. During that session the legislature also killed every salary increase for teachers that was introduced.

Teachers found little, if any, solace locally. In some counties, particularly in the northern tier, citizens' groups like the Freeholders Association lobbied against any tax increase they could find. In Escambia County when the school board attempted to apprise voters of serious educational needs (chalk, buildings, textbooks, equipment, and reading resources), the Freeholders used every means available—radio, TV, speakers, news releases, and the like—to convince the public that any money voted for schools wouldn't be properly utilized.

The Freeholders claimed that funds voted by the taxpayers for schools would never get to the students. By this, they meant that any tax increase would go toward superfluous things like salaries for teachers and administrators. This kind of mugging was not unique to Escambia County by any means; other counties in north and central Florida faced the same problem. The attitude expressed by many citizens in Florida's low tax culture was often mindless and automatic: "We already pay enough taxes; let 'em cut back somewhere."

All of these indignities exacerbated the increasing frustration of the state's teachers, and that frustration was reaching critical mass. Sick and tired of bogus promises, political cravenness, financial neglect, and the lack of public support, their frustration finally slipped past the point of no return. For most teachers, any hope of making improvements in education—like expanding the kindergarten program into more counties, or providing adequate resources for special education programs, or upgrading obsolete textbooks, or reducing horrendous class sizes, or improving teachers' salaries, or getting needed classroom supplies—was growing more and more dim.

As teachers reached the end of their professional patience, they turned increasingly to FEA for help. The organization was compelled to do something, particularly since its ongoing efforts with the governor, the legislature, and the cabinet had gone practically nowhere. Yet, what could FEA really do to help its beleaguered members? Without a collective bargaining law, neither FEA nor its locals could force those in power to treat teachers as equals in remedying problems related to salaries or working conditions. Without such a vehicle for meaningful give-and-take on these issues, frustration was left unchecked.

The issue of teacher morale was of transcending importance in the education crisis of 1967–1968. As much as any other factor, it led to the statewide walkout that year. It wasn't just that the Florida power structure took the teachers' enduring patience for granted, it was that *they counted on it.* Florida's teachers had lost hope, and the State of Florida was sitting on a powder keg of its own making.

As history has demonstrated time on end, previously docile, even phlegmatic, constituencies often rebel when hope is lost; yet, the state continued to offer teachers nothing to assuage their fading hope and legitimate concerns. During the buildup to the strike, several legislators told FEA leaders that if teachers in Florida weren't happy with the way things were they should pack up and leave the state. Comments like those served only to encourage the tsunami of teacher resentment that was washing over the state.

By the summer of 1967, Florida's teachers had finally had enough of it all: the patronization, the bullying, the parsimony, the trivialization of real problems, the dismissive attitudes, and even their own historic acquiescence.

As Albert Finney's character shouted from his office window in the movie *Network,* "I'm mad as hell and I'm not going to take it any more," Florida's teachers were mad as hell, and they weren't going to take it any more. Teachers were ready to do something, and during the months leading up to the strike FEA ran frenetically to keep in front of its own membership.

Things between FEA and the power structure had heated up considerably in the spring of 1967 when the Democrat majority in the legislature passed education appropriation bills totaling about $130 million, much of which was to be paid for with a series of nuisance taxes on cigarettes, whiskey, and beer. While FEA did not consider the appropriation to be adequate by any stretch, the issue became moot when Governor Kirk vetoed the provisions because they required an increase in taxes.

Unfortunately, Kirk had enough Republican support in the legislature to ensure that his veto would not be overridden. Being able to count on Republican support was an important piece of business for the governor because his use of the veto became a dominant part of his dealings with the Democrat-controlled legislature. His hair-trigger vetoes also exacerbated his relationship with FEA. In any event, the 1967 legislature adjourned in April without an education budget.

For several months, FEA had been warning Florida officials that if education conditions did not improve, FEA would impose "sanctions" on the state. Sanctions were a devise utilized by the FEA and NEA to call national attention to unacceptable educational conditions in a state or local community. If imposed on the State of Florida, sanctions would censure the state government and discourage educators across America from taking a job anywhere in the Florida education system.

With the threat of sanctions hanging over its head, the Florida legislature extended its session into June and continued to fight with the governor over funding issues. Trying to reach a compromise with Kirk, the legislature put forward several proposals, all of which he rejected. Finally, on June 29 Kirk unilaterally wrote his own budget by utilizing his line-item veto power. In doing so, he cut $164 million in appropriations, about $150 million of which had been earmarked for education.

Of course, FEA denounced Kirk's budget, but it became law when the Republicans in the legislature again refused to override his vetoes. The unilateral and arrogant action of the governor enraged many Democrat legislators and virtually all of the state's educators, and FEA began to have trouble keeping the lid on the anger boiling within its ranks. Because of the governor's vetoes of the education appropriations, and because of the state's long history of educational neglect, on May 25, 1967, FEA imposed sanctions on the state and asked the National Education Association to do likewise. NEA followed suit on June 5, 1967.

With teacher frustration mounting by the hour, and local associations demanding action, the pot did, indeed, boil over. By August 11, Pinellas County teachers had had enough. Their executive secretary, Larry Black, stated, "We are not willing to wait any more. We are fed up with waiting for the next year, the next legislative session."[6] After voting 1,555 to 222 to go on strike, they went out.

The Pinellas school board quickly obtained an injunction ordering the teachers back to work, and they reluctantly returned to their classrooms on August 17. However, over 2,000 Pinellas County teachers had signed resignation forms and handed them to their local association leaders; they threatened to go out again if positive things didn't begin to happen.

Three weeks later, on September 5, about 2,400 Broward County teachers, under the leadership of that county's teacher association president Marge Head, went on strike and closed down the Broward County schools for over a week. The teachers returned after getting a small pay raise and assurances from the school board that it would support a special session of the legislature. In return, Broward County teachers agreed in the settlement not to support a statewide strike if one was called by FEA.

A few months later in northern Florida (hardly a breeding ground of teacher militancy) Clay County teachers struck on December 7 over low salaries and pay cuts imposed by the school board. Over 700 of the 763 teachers went out and didn't return until December 13. Teachers in Dade, Duval, and Hillsborough Counties were also threatening to strike. Things were getting serious.

FEA tried to cool things down, or at least keep everything coordinated. It designated October 1, 1967 as "Crisis Sunday" so that teachers across the state could invite citizens to their schools to see the deteriorating conditions for themselves and discuss the teachers' concerns. Attendance by parents and other citizens around the state was mostly sparse, which severely disappointed the teachers.

In addition to Crisis Sunday, FEA pushed for the governor to call a special session of the legislature, one devoted exclusively to education. Governor Kirk, however, refused to commit to a special session and issued combative threats about no new taxes, which only served to further poison the atmosphere. FEA also ratcheted up its rhetoric, with Phil Constans, FEA's charismatic executive secretary, taking the lead.

To make certain that it was accurately reflecting the mood and direction of its membership, FEA asked teachers from around the state to attend a one-day meeting at the Tangerine Bowl in Orlando on August 14, 1967. Worried about how many teachers would show up, Constans and George Dabbs, FEA's communications director and former FEA president, had arranged for FEA cameras to focus only on one small section of the stands if the turnout should be meager. They need not have worried.

Well over 35,000 teachers descended on the Tangerine Bowl that August day to vent their anger and show solidarity. They not only filled the stands to capacity, they jammed the entire infield. Hundreds had to listen to the proceedings outside the stadium on the loudspeakers. Many wore tangerine-colored buttons that read: "Be There." Because of the tremendous traffic tie-ups caused by the size of the crowd, some teachers never even made it to the meeting. By any standard, the meeting was a huge success, which not only emboldened FEA but also sent a tremor through the ranks of Florida's elected officials.

Teachers didn't just show up; they made it clear to FEA's leaders that they wanted action. If Constans had asked them that day to strike, as many of those who attended had anticipated he would, there is not a shred of doubt they would have gone out on whatever date was set. Constans, however, wanting to give Kirk and the legislature a little more time, pleaded for even more patience from the irate throng.

In his speech to the energized crowd, he implored, "While I savor the pride of this moment, I must turn on the other hand to my assignment; and it is not an easy one. I am compelled to ask you to do something that many of you do not want to do. I am going to suggest that you do something which requires deliberate and individual strength and courage. On this day I must ask you to turn the other cheek—to go the extra mile—to try again. I am suggesting that you place your resignation in the hands of your elected leadership. And I implore you not to take this matter lightly."[7]

Constans and FEA were buying time to get the special session of the legislature, time to alert and educate Floridians about the impending crisis, and time to work out some kind of agreement with the governor and/or legislature. FEA was willing to pull the trigger if necessary, but it wanted to avoid a statewide walkout if at all possible. After the Tangerine Bowl turnout, there was no doubt in anyone's mind that the possibility of a statewide strike was more than an idle boast or empty threat. In fact, after the meeting, Governor Kirk's aides began to discuss a settlement of the funding issues in a much more serious tone.

Phil Constans was successful in his effort to convince the impatient and frustrated Tangerine Bowl crowd to wait a little longer. They were willing to do so because they had previously developed faith in him and his eloquent calls for unity and determination. FEA was fortunate to have Constans as its leader. He had become the Florida Education Association's executive secretary in 1967 when he was just thirty-nine years old.

Dr. Constans had received his doctorate from the University of Florida, and before joining the FEA staff in 1966, had been a principal at a Cocoa Beach high school. Constans had served a term as FEA president in 1958 and, when appointed FEA executive secretary, had succeeded Ed Henderson, a much more conservative leader who had held the office for over eighteen years.

Constans not only mirrored the growing militancy of the FEA members, he gave eloquent voice to it. Teachers admired and respected Constans because he didn't speak *to* them, he spoke *for* them, and he shared their frustration. He was a dynamic and effective leader and speaker who combined a keen intellect with his ability to rouse an audience. He knew how to get a crowd to its feet, but he never used hyperbole or histrionics to draw attention to himself and away from the issues he was emphasizing. As far as FEA members were concerned, he was the right leader for the right time . . . and the time was right.

Governor Kirk continued to vacillate about calling a special legislative session even as pressure from FEA, his own cabinet, and some legislators mounted. Instead, in October 1967 he tried to deflect attention by announcing he would move up the date for a report from his previously appointed Quality Education Commission, ordering the report to be available by the Christmas holidays. FEA quickly pledged its cooperation by holding all sanctions in abeyance while the report was being compiled.

FEA also offered research and staff assistance to the Commission with the hope that its findings would serve as a catalyst for resolving the crisis. The Commission's report came out in December but was ineffectual in resolving the issues or abating the crisis. FEA thought it had a commitment from the governor to take the Commission's recommendations to a special session of the legislature for adoption.

Kirk claimed that he never made such a commitment and wasn't even sure he was going to call a special session. (Kirk had a habit of providing commitments in private only to change his mind if the political winds kicked up; he would feign never having made such a commitment. His contretemps with the Republicans in the legislature over pay raises was another example of this ploy.)

With FEA considering another mass rally of teachers to begin some kind of action, Kirk finally called a special ten-day session of the legislature to begin on January 29. During that session the Senate passed an education bill acceptable to FEA, but the House–Senate Conference Committee not only cut expenditures from the original bill, it went on to reallocate revenues previously earmarked for education to noneducation items.

The education package totaled $250 million in additional funds for education to be paid for through a series of nuisance taxes. With a resolution of the crisis staring him in the face, the governor promised to veto the bill because it did not provide for a referendum on the new taxes.

FEA also opposed the bill as it finally appeared because funds had been cut in the conference committee and because revenues earmarked for education had been set aside for noneducation purposes. There ensued a protracted dispute about just how much of the $250 million would actually go to education. Ironically, the special session produced a bill that turned out to be unacceptable to both FEA and the governor for entirely different reasons.

On February 16 the special session of the legislature adjourned without the crisis being resolved. To this day, many former FEA leaders and staff believe that if Kirk had signed off on the special sessions package, FEA would have followed suit. However, with Kirk threatening to veto the package as he had done many times before, FEA had every reason to expect him to do so again. To Florida's teachers, the whole episode was but one more example of the education system burning while Kirk and the legislature fiddled.

As far as FEA was concerned, it had run out of time with the governor, the legislature, and its own members. Action became the only viable option. On Friday, February 16, FEA announced that it was activating over 35,000 resignations to go into effect on Monday, February 19. After years of frustration, the trigger had been pulled.

5

THE WALKOUT

On February 19, 1968, 35,000 valorous men and women teachers walked off their jobs in Florida. After years of being ignored and patronized, and with Florida education continuing to disintegrate, teachers had finally crossed their personal and collective Rubicon. Forced into a corner, they came to the conclusion that their only viable alternative was to confront the establishment.

When Florida's teachers walked out, they experienced the high of being together in large numbers and standing up for what they believed to be important for Florida's children. They were, however, also gripped with crippling uncertainty and fear, not only for themselves, but for their families as well. The strike had a profound impact on each individual participant. It is difficult for those who didn't live through the experience to fathom the depth of the angst that accompanied each striking teacher as they went out the door.

The standard resignation form signed by each individual teacher read as follows:

> *Dear* _____:
> *I hereby request that the Board of Public Instruction accept my resignation from employment in the public school system of this county to be effective as of the date of the next regular meeting of the Board.*
>
> *I can no longer render professional services to an agency of Florida government which the public, through its elected officials, does not support in a responsible manner. I believe this fact constitutes good and sufficient cause for this request for release from the contract of employment.*
> *Respectfully,* _____

A plethora of thoughts bounced back and forth in the minds of the teachers who signed and turned in those resignation forms. While they were proud to stand up and be counted, they knew they had resigned their jobs without any legal protection whatsoever. They also expected the entire state's power structure to align against them. They weighed a hundred considerations and analyzed a thousand possibilities before exiting their schoolhouse doors.

What would such an act mean legally, they wondered? Would they go to jail? What would the impact be on their families? Already financially pinched, how would they cope with financial losses? What would their students think? What about their parents? What would the teachers' parents and relatives think? What would happen to their collegial relationships with those in their building who didn't strike? What about their building principal? On and on the questions went.

Mary Stanley was an English and Spanish teacher at Clubbs Junior High in Pensacola, and a typical striking teacher. She had two small children and was helping her husband through law school at the time of the walkout. She said she struck because she had confidence in her building principal, Fred Haushaulter, who was also an association leader, and because teachers needed better salaries. From the first day of the walkout, Mary was "scared to death—petrified" of losing her job and income. Nevertheless, she not only stayed out, but also worked continually to bolster friends who were weakening.[1]

Bea Griswold taught at Cross Bayou School in Pinellas County. She and another teacher taught two classes together in the same room, about sixty kids together with no air conditioning. She went out to get "a better shake" for the kids she taught. Bea remembers being a member of the "Resigners Club" in Pinellas. Each walkout teacher carried a card that sported an alligator clad in a cap and gown and holding a diploma. The card read: "Bea Griswold is a member of the Resigners Club. The Resigners are Florida educators who, for the first time in the history of the United States, jointly resigned their positions as educators so that the children of Florida would be assured quality education."[2]

Florida's striking teachers were no different than teachers everywhere else in America. They loved children, especially their own students. They were somewhat idealistic and often selfless. They were largely nonpolitical. They were not anarchists; nor were they subversives. They weren't radicals or Communists. They weren't really unionists. And, confrontation didn't come easy to them. Some of those doing the confronting were young, fresh-faced rookies on probation and without tenure, feeling their way through their first year in the classroom. Some were wizened veterans who had been looking forward to crossing the finish line and retirement. Some were administrators: principals and central office personnel who felt personally obliged to stand with their striking colleagues.

Some were African American teachers who had suffered slights and indignities well beyond those of their white colleagues. Black teachers were just beginning to be integrated into the public school system after years of dalliance by the State of Florida following the 1954 *Brown v. Board of Education* Supreme Court decision.

They were elementary school teachers, junior high teachers, senior high school teachers, community college teachers, and administrators. Despite their trepidation, most of them understood exactly what was going on and viewed the issues clearly. Others were a little foggy on the state-level issues, but keenly aware of the issues that faced them in their classroom. Some were just fed up, and relied on their colleagues, friends, and FEA leaders to analyze the big picture for them.

In some counties, mothers and daughters not only taught together, but also went on strike together (there were a few father-son combinations as well). Many couples who were both teaching went out side by side. On the other hand, some households were wracked by spousal conflict over the walkout, and more than a few marriages ended in divorce.

For almost all the strikers, going without even one paycheck was likely to be devastating. The record is replete with instances of single parents who could ill afford to miss a single payday. Some, in addition to their own financial burdens, served as health-care providers for an ill child or parent. The bottom line was that very few of those who went out could afford to miss one day of work, let alone weeks. Most of them had no earthly idea how they would survive financially. Many had to borrow money from friends or relatives, and some even had to move in with them.

With few exceptions, most of those who went out had never participated in a work stoppage before, or broken the law, or gambled with their family's security. This was new territory, and the strikers had no idea what to expect. They struck without the protection of labor statutes or even the comfort of precedent in Florida or anywhere else. They stepped out of their school buildings into a dark and intimidating abyss.

It would be difficult for teachers to take such a risk today, but the courage that it took to make that leap of faith in 1968 was nothing short of staggering. The fortitude required to join the statewide walkout was bolstered only by the unadulterated belief that they were doing something noble and necessary. By participating, they took part in the most daring event most of them had ever experienced, or ever would. They opened their hearts, closed their eyes, and jumped.

Despite their great diversity of race, gender, school setting, and political views, virtually all those who walked out of their classrooms in February 1968 shared three common characteristics: they were distressed at the deteriorating state of Florida's education system; they were loyal members of FEA who at least had each other to lean on; and they were petrified. In any event, they considered themselves on a mission for the children of Florida, and they walked out with the breathless conviction that they would make a positive difference.

While they realized that what they were doing was unprecedented and dangerous, they also knew that continuing tacitly to endorse a subpar education for their students was wrong. Their quest was, at the same time, Quixotic and grounded, clear-eyed and naive, hardheaded and emotional.

As frustrated as Florida's teachers were about their own low salaries, they were much more concerned about how their students were being shortchanged. Forty years after the event, they continue to express that same conviction. The passage of four decades may have played havoc with their bodies—and perhaps their lives—but the idealism that drove them in 1968 hasn't waned.

On that February day in 1968, Florida classrooms were drained of their teachers the length and breadth of the peninsula. Schools emptied at both ends of the panhandle: from Duval County in the Florida's northeast corner all the way over to Escambia County in the far northwest. Teachers struck in Dade and Monroe Counties at the state's foot, as well as Orange, Polk, and Highlands Counties in the state's interior. They struck in Pinellas and Hillsborough Counties on the west coast, and across the peninsula to Brevard and Volusia Counties on the east coast. They went out in Collier County in the southwest and all the way across Alligator Alley to Palm Beach and Broward Counties in the southeast.

Schools were forced to close immediately and entirely in twenty-two of the state's sixty-seven counties, with most of the other counties struggling to keep some schools open. Only about half of the state's teachers participated in the walkout, which meant that the entire Florida public school system never did close down. That was problematic for FEA, and so was the fact that other school employees like secretaries, bus drivers, cafeteria workers, and so forth were never part of the walkout. In other words, not enough schools closed to make the strike a roaring success, but enough were shuttered to give validity to the effort.

Phil Constans being served with a subpoena in Leon County (1968)

From Left to Right: Phil Constans, FEA Executive Secretary; Braulio Alonzo, NEA
President; Dexter Hogman, FEA President (1968)

Phil Constans at a Tangerine Bowl Rally (August 1967)

Phil Constans Speaking at a Tangerine Bowl Rally (August 1967)

Phil Constans, FEA Executive Secretary (1968)

From Left to Right: Phil Constans, FEA Executive Secretary; Braulio Alonzo, NEA President; Dexter Hogman, FEA President at a presentation event (1968).

Phil Constans and FEA Leaders

Teacher Rally at Tangerine Bowl (August 1967)

Teacher Crowd at Tangerine Bowl (August 1967)

Phil Constans Speaking into Microphone at Tangerine Bowl Rally (August 1967)

From Left to Right: Phil Constans, FEA Executive Secretary; Governor Claude Kirk, Governor of Florida; Dexter Hogman, FEA President

Governor Claude Kirk (1968)

From Left to Right: Cecil Hauman, NEA Staff; Floyd Christian, Florida Commissioner of Education; Dexter Hogman, FEA President (1968)

Having some schools open or partially open proved to be a boon to local school boards because they were able to hire temporary "replacement" teachers. Some community businesses even paid their employees to become replacement teachers. Most of the replacements, or "scabs," as the teachers correctly called them, served little educational purpose, but they did provide a warm body in the front of the classroom. Many of the replacements had no earthly idea what they were doing or how to maintain student discipline. By any standard, very little education took place in the classrooms staffed with replacement teachers. Floyd Christian said, "We are keeping school, but we are not teaching school."[3]

Much to the consternation of striking teachers, some of the replacements turned out to be their neighbors, friends, and even relatives. At one of the daily meetings in a northern tier county, a teacher told of being replaced by her neighbor. In Pasco County, Jim Geiger and his wife Sharon, a first grade teacher, who were both on strike, had the experience of seeing Sharon replaced in her classroom by the wife of their family doctor, a close friend who had given them a bottle of champagne on their wedding day eighteen months earlier.[4] Also in Pasco County, a high school teacher with almost thirty years' experience was replaced by one of her former students.

To understand more fully why a band of rebellious neophyte teachers would walk off their jobs for anywhere from three to six weeks, their action must be viewed in the context of what they were feeling. To skip that context would not serve history well, and it would do a disservice to those teachers who put their jobs on the line.

As related earlier, the walkout burst onto the scene with the impact of a tropical storm, but it didn't suddenly materialize in an otherwise sunny Florida sky. Indeed, storm clouds had been gathering on the educational horizon for a long time, and thunderclaps of alarm had been cascading around the state for at least a decade. To Florida's teachers, the strike was the culmination of a long string of broken promises, broken faith, and broken trust between them and the State of Florida. After a hundred years of patience, it had become abundantly clear to Florida's teachers that passivity and compliance had produced very little for them or their students.

Quite the contrary, acquiescence had served no purpose except to whittle away their ability to teach and to crush their morale; it also negatively impacted their students' ability to learn. As far as the striking teachers were concerned, waiting for school boards and legislators to do the right thing hadn't worked, and it became clear to them that it wasn't going to work in the future either. They came to accept the finality that the repeated promises politicians made to them were nothing more than delaying tactics at best, and meaningless lies at worst.

Once the strike occurred, it ushered in a three- to six-week maelstrom of accusations, recriminations, confusion, and turmoil within the State of Florida. It marked the first time in the nation's history that public school teachers had walked off their jobs statewide for more than a day or so of symbolic protest, and it focused national attention on the negligent stewardship of the Florida power structure. No one, let alone teachers, had ever challenged Florida's legislature, governor, and business lobby head-on before. They had called the Good Ol' Boys and the state's low tax obsession to account.

The striking teachers not only had faith in their mission, they also had faith in their Association leaders. Teachers knew that the organization leaders they had elected wouldn't sell them a bill of goods. They knew and trusted them, particularly at the local level. In Pensacola, to cite but one of many examples, several former striking teachers recently claimed that back in 1968 if their president, Fred Haushaulter, had told them that swimming across Escambia Bay would solve the education crisis, they'd have waded in. The same could be said of others leaders like Bob Martinez in Hillsborough County, Pat Tornillo in Dade County, Larry Black in Pinellas County, and Marge Head in Broward County, to name but a few.

The best known and most controversial of the local leaders was Pat Tornillo in Dade County. The Dade Classroom Teachers Association was already a powerful force in state educational politics, and by the time of the walkout Tornillo had become a mover and shaker in the teacher union movement in Florida.

Tornillo began his career as a teacher in New Jersey but came to Florida in 1956 to teach in Dade County. He became an activist in the Dade Classroom Teachers Association and became its senior vice president in 1962. The pugnacious leader, known for his short stature and combative tactics, was a throwback to union leaders of decades earlier. Accused of many things over the years, he was never accused of shying away from either a fight or a television camera.

Tornillo's greatest accomplishments for Florida unionism were twofold: his push for civil rights and integration, and his long-standing advocacy for a collective bargaining statute for Florida public employees. He and his local president, Janet Dean, were front-line players in the effort to get both FEA and NEA to become more aggressive in representing their members. FEA's Dade County local was, in many ways, the lynchpin for the 1968 strike because its 9,000 members added a powerful component to FEA's confrontation with the Florida power structure.

The Florida Education Association called the 1968 statewide strike only after months of pleading, cajoling, threatening, and warning those in authority and anyone else who would listen. Of prime importance, however, is the fact that the 35,000 teachers who went out didn't just strike. They resigned. They had literally turned in their signed resignations to the school authorities.

Phil Constans and other FEA leaders today acknowledge that they made a serious error by going the resignation route. Constans says that they took the advice given to them by their nonlabor attorney at the time. The lawyer advised them that resigning en masse could obviate the state's ban on strikes by public employees. In retrospect, the resignation tactic not only failed to circumvent the legal issue, but it placed the striking teachers in the rather vulnerable position of having voluntarily unemployed themselves.

That being the case, the resignations put every individual teacher at the mercy of their local school board when it came time to return to work. At the conclusion of the strike, some school boards were, in fact, exceedingly vindictive. The mass resignations strategy could only have worked if FEA had been in control of when and under what conditions all its members returned to their classrooms. It wasn't.

The adoption of the resignation strategy was a reflection of FEA's inexperience as a union. In 1968 FEA was, and had been since its inception, anything but a union per se. It was part of the National Education Association's state affiliate network of "professional associations" that were administrator-dominated and opposed to teachers being represented by organized labor. Until the 1960s, those associations were more in tune with the education establishment (superintendents, administrators, state commissioners of education, school boards, and the like) than with the teachers in the classroom even though those teachers comprised 90 percent of their memberships.

FEA's foray into utilizing union tactics (such as striking) was born of necessity, not philosophy. For over eighty years FEA had not involved itself in electoral politics, collective bargaining, striking, boycotting, or any other activities designed to challenge the status quo. It lobbied for increased education funding and that was about it. The bottom line is that FEA jumped into rough seas to save Florida education and its own members even though it could barely swim itself.

If it had not been for four factors that came into play, FEA could easily have drowned as an organization in those rough seas. The first factor, without question, was the determination and courage of the striking teachers. The second was the massive assistance provided by NEA to Florida even though it was less than enthusiastic about the strike, and even while it was in the throes of an internal union-professional association-wrestling match of its own. The third factor was the credible work of FEA leaders and staff, aided by NEA staff, in organizing such a huge venture. The role played by the large Florida locals in this regard was extremely important. And fourth, the leadership of Phil Constans was a strong, unifying factor.

From the first day of the strike, FEA thought it knew what it was up against, but that was not entirely the case. FEA certainly didn't take the strike action lightly or without serious analysis, but it was operating on some shaky assumptions. For example, it was assumed that, as with most strikes in America, the adversarial parties would ultimately hammer out a mutual resolution to the conflict. Unfortunately, that assumption hinged on an even shakier one: that there existed in Florida an adversary that was interested in seeking mutual resolution.

While some members of the legislature and cabinet, most notably Ralph Turlington, speaker of the House of Representatives, and Floyd Christian, state superintendent of public instruction, were certainly interested in mutual resolution of the crisis, Governor Claude Roy Kirk was not. The governor, with the support of most Republican legislators, wanted resolution only on his own terms and only if he could be publicly crowned as victorious. He was an implacable obstacle to compromise and resolution.

Kirk publicly treated the education crisis as a kind of pesky irritant. Just before the strike began, he was quoted as saying that there was no education crisis in Florida. It was more than symbolic that the day 35,000 Florida teachers chose to leave their jobs to protest the sad state of education, Governor Kirk chose to be out of the state on a political junket. On February 19, the first day of the strike, photographers snapped Kirk's picture at California's Disneyland shaking hands with Goofy.[5]

6

RETRIBUTION

Once the strike began, various components of the power structure across the state used all kinds of tactics to get teachers to defect from FEA's ranks and return to work. Those tactics included injunctions, threats of immediate dismissal and decertification, and having students call teachers at home to urge their return to the classroom. Even reclassifying young male teachers to make them eligible for the draft and a trip to Vietnam was not out of bounds.

Some male teachers were, indeed, reclassified, drafted, and sent to combat in Vietnam. On a Monday morning in one of the daily meetings in a central Florida county, two young couples were talking in a corner of the auditorium; both women were crying. On the previous Friday the men had been called by their draft board and told that if they weren't back in school on Monday morning they would be reclassified 1-A. The two couples had spent the weekend together talking and praying, and had finally decided to remain on strike.[1]

It was not unusual for preachers to denounce the strike from the pulpit, and it was fairly common for striking teachers to skip Sunday worship because of the comments made to them by fellow members of their parish, temple, or congregation. Sometimes parents of high school seniors accused them of being responsible for their son or daughter not being able to graduate in the spring.

In Hernando County, at the beginning of the strike, the school board threatened to revoke the teaching certificate of any striking teacher who wasn't back in the classroom in two hours. In Broward County, at the conclusion of the strike, over sixty teachers were decertified and prohibited from teaching in Florida. Many of them went to other states to teach, including BCTA's president, Marge Head, who left to teach in Hattiesburg, Mississippi.

Many teachers were taken from the school where they had taught prior to the strike and plopped down in another school, sometimes teaching out of their subject area. The vast majority of principals who went out with the teachers were fired, demoted, or transferred.

In Sarasota County, a young female teacher's husband threatened to divorce her if she walked out, which she was determined to do. She and her husband had also been arguing for some time about her strong desire to have a child, which he adamantly refused to consider. On the day of the walkout, she informed her colleagues that she would not be going out with them. Two months later, she announced that she was pregnant.[2] A coincidence?

Every striking teacher has a story to tell, and every story is different. In Suwannee County, Barbara DeVane was a second year probationary teacher. In the fall of 1967, just months prior to the walkout, she and her Suwannee colleagues were called together so that a board of education member could explain to them why the school board was going to reduce their salaries by 11 percent.

DeVane knew from a friend who worked inside the administration that the real reason teacher salaries were to be cut was that the administration had made a mistake in its reporting to the state about the number of students attending classes and the district would therefore not receive the funding from the state it had budgeted. In other words, the school system was going to force its already grossly underpaid teachers to subsidize its own clerical mistake and concocted a story to cover itself. In the meeting, DeVane exposed the real cause for the pay cut—as opposed to the fictitious one offered by the school board member. During the resulting exchange, she said that the board member was telling a "bare-faced lie."

Shortly after the meeting, DeVane's building principal told her that she was suspended from teaching. Within a few days she received a letter from the school board demanding that she apologize to the board. The letter admonished her to report to a board hearing where she was to be charged with immorality, gross misconduct, and behavior unbecoming a teacher. The board was claiming that she had called its member a "bare-assed liar" during the teachers' meeting (a claim proven to be false).

DeVane not only refused to apologize, but also got FEA legal help in preparing for the upcoming December board hearing. Just before the hearing was to take place, she received another letter from the school board *apologizing to her* and directing her to report back to work. The letter also gratuitously asked her to behave herself for the rest of the year. She reported back to work, but two short months later she walked off her job along with the rest of the striking Florida teachers.[3]

What happened in Suwannee County is reflective of the dismissive attitude that school boards and the legislature held toward teachers' salaries. Florida's legislature was being no less disingenuous than the Suwannee County board when it continually offered bogus reasons to FEA and its teacher members for not funding salaries properly. When the veneer of excuses was stripped away, teachers were being asked to subsidize the errors and omissions of the State of Florida with their own meager salaries.

On another front, the negative reaction by much of the public (not all) surprised most teachers. In many communities, particularly in the northern part of the state, those who walked out were charged with all kinds of ulterior motives. They were spit at, subjected to verbal epithets, and accused of being everything from Communists to the anti-Christ. Jane Arnold, FEA president in 1968–1969, said, "We thought the public would be with us. We thought it would unite the community and the teachers. It did a little bit of the opposite. A lot of teachers lost their innocence because they thought the community liked them."[4]

For his part, commenting twenty years later, Claude Kirk Jr. had his own view about this phenomenon. He claimed that, "The total pressure [on me] to stop the strike was that mom and dad didn't want Johnny at home. They said, 'Get that kid back in school because he's in my way.'"[5]

Don Treadwell, who lives in northwest Florida, remembers what happened with his dad during the strike. "My father was one of the brave teachers who walked out in 1968. He was teaching in Holmes County, where only a small percentage of teachers resigned, and those who did were ostracized by many in the community. My dad and his brother, also a teacher, were red baited—accused of being in league with the 'Communist FEA'—in the weekly newspaper by the superintendent. After the strike teachers in Holmes County were required to sign a pledge not to discuss the walkout after they returned to work. My dad refused to sign and instead left the county where he and my mother were born and raised."[6]

The name-calling that many striking teachers endured was especially hurtful because there was nothing in their background or training to prepare them for such abuse. They weren't experienced community rabble-rousers or ne'er-do-wells. They were teachers of Florida's children who were concerned about the quality of the education system and decided to stage a protest. They were poorly paid professionals who lived and worked in the same neighborhoods as the name-callers.

A common charge leveled against FEA was that the "union bosses" and "loudmouths" were forcing gullible teachers to comply with union goals. Another common accusation was that the strike was conceived and orchestrated by "outsiders" who were pushing a national union agenda. Larry Sorensen, a staffer assigned to Florida during the strike by NEA, attended one of the daily strike briefings in Okaloosa County. Upon returning to his motel room, his key wouldn't work. When he went to check at the office, he saw that his bags were packed and sitting on the office floor. When he asked what was going on, the proprietor snarled, "We don't have rooms available for troublemakers from the outside." Sorensen had to find new digs.

Typical of the inanities being promulgated around the state was the following syndicated column by James J. Kilpatrick, a well-known, conservative commentator:

> Most of the deficiencies that the Florida Education Association deplored—the overcrowded classrooms, leaky roofs, outdated textbooks, rickety buses—were on their way toward correction before the strike began. The gut issue came straight from the traditions of trade unionism. The FEA was seeking recognition as the exclusive bargaining agent for all the state's teachers, principals and supervisors. To that end, FEA had proposed a system that might have been drawn fresh from the files of the Teamsters Union. On that issue, the striking teachers lost.[7]

Such accusations were not only self-serving and patronizing, but they stood truth on its head. Teacher militancy in Florida most assuredly did not come from outside agitators. For its part, the National Education Association had not been an enthusiastic booster of the Florida strike in the first place. AFL-CIO unions, such as the American Federation of Teachers, were certainly not stirring the pot in Florida. The Florida strike was homegrown and local from beginning to end, and was spawned entirely within the bleak educational atmosphere created by that state's political leaders

It wasn't only the media that railed against striking teachers. The business interests in Florida publicly engaged in opposing the strike. Groups like Associated Industries and the Chamber of Commerce fought bitterly against the striking teachers. They were, of course, opposed to any teacher pay raises or educational improvements that would cause taxes to increase.

Associated Industries of Florida was particularly vitriolic in its fulminations against the teachers. The members of Associated Industries stuck their collective noses into the conflict in a fashion unprecedented in other states. Associated Industries went so far as to send a letter to the Florida Cabinet members urging them to fire all 35,000 striking teachers. In part, the letter read: "It is far better to endure pain briefly now while effecting a cure than to allow a cancerous growth to erode our basic system of government."[8]

The letter was not only venomous in its nature, it was malevolent in its intent. It did, however, pull back the curtain to reveal the role that industry had always played in running Florida's affairs. The missive was no less revealing in its attribution to "our" system of government. Who exactly was "our?" It surely wasn't anyone who gave a damn about educational quality, students, or teachers. The letter demonstrated for all to see how the Florida power structure viewed public service generally, and education in particular.

From one end of Florida to the other, the business community, large and small, opposed the teacher walkout. Because of that active opposition, FEA locals all over the state had difficulty securing meeting places for the teachers' daily briefings. In Sarasota, the local association had to rent space in a movie theater because all the regular meeting venues were closed to them.

According to Phil Constans, "We had a terrible time keeping places to meet. In some localities, such as Tampa, it became a real contest as to whether we could find meeting places faster than they were taken away. In Monroe County the teachers first met in the old city hall. After one meeting, this was no longer available to them. However, they found refuge in the Church of the Rock. Next day, I was informed that the Rock had crumbled. We moved these teachers to Miami and had them meet with the Dade teachers after that."[9]

Local merchants in many communities refused to extend credit to striking teachers, making them pay cash for whatever they purchased. Ruth Holmes, at that time a striking teacher in Pensacola, tells the story of going into a local pharmacy to get a prescription filled for her sick child. The owner, who had been doing business with her and her parents for many years, asked how she intended to pay for the prescription. When Ruth asked why, she was told that since she was on strike credit would not be available to her. She promptly took her prescription back, told the pharmacy owner that she would take her business elsewhere (adding a choice phrase or two), and never set foot in that pharmacy again.[10]

Local businesses around the state ran newspaper adds castigating the striking teachers, offering support to the local board of education, and listing the names of businesses in town (banks, stores, and services) that were opposed to the strike. In Escambia, to demonstrate support for the Board of Education and opposition to the striking teachers, prominent business leaders from the local Chamber of Commerce attended a school board meeting during the strike and literally stood, facing the audience, behind each school board member.[11] Teachers had no difficulty getting the message.

There were, to be sure, some business people who were not hostile, but even supportive. In Pasco County the owner of Marston's Turkeyland, one of Florida's largest turkey farms, donated three hundred turkeys to the teachers so they wouldn't go hungry. Individual community professionals and business executives occasionally voiced support. In Suwannee a telephone company regional manager attended several of the teacher meetings to offer assistance and support.

In Duval, Bill Maness, a prominent lawyer to a large company in the county, attended a strike meeting and spoke in support of the teachers. He was quoted in the *Florida Times Union* encouraging teachers to stick to their guns. Subsequently, Maness was called into the CEO's office and ordered to retract his statement in the newspaper. He refused to do so, and resigned his job with the company.

Encouragement and overt support came from individuals in many counties, but that was certainly not the case with almost all the vested business organizations. They remained steadfastly and unalterably opposed to the strike, the striking teachers, and the goals they sought.

In the face of this kind of intense and ever-escalating pressure, the measure of the striking teachers was taken virtually every day, forcing them to reexamine their motives and their resolve. As the strike went into its second and third weeks, defections from the ranks increased because of the pressure. For those who remained out, the courage that it took to withstand the pressure became severe and, in some cases, almost unbearable.

7

THE STRIKE COLLAPSES

A s the strike wore on, the Florida Cabinet, led by Floyd Christian and without Governor Kirk's participation, tried to craft a compromise that would end the strike, but Kirk scuttled the effort. He publicly chastised the cabinet and the proposal, saying that it was drawn without his involvement (which it was), that it gave collective bargaining to the union (which it didn't), and that it took power away from the people and gave it to the teachers union (untrue and pure hyperbole).

In his zeal to bury the compromise, Kirk enlisted the support of local school boards, which were antiunion to begin with, and also went public with his message. Due to the governor's fusillade, Christian's initiative to reach accord with FEA went down in flames. This incident not only reflected on Kirk's refusals to compromise with FEA, it also exposed his animus toward his cabinet and Floyd Christian.

Finally, after three grinding weeks, on March 7, 1968 the strike ended for most teachers amid considerable confusion and consternation. That's the day the package approved by the special session of the legislature became law without Governor Kirk's signature. The following day, on March 8, FEA called the strike off, but its problems were far from over.

FEA found that as difficult as it had been to take the state's teachers out on strike, it was exponentially more difficult to get them all back in safely. This circumstance came about because there was never a mutually negotiated agreement between the power structure (the governor, legislature, and school boards) and FEA that codified the terms for ending the walkout.

There was no traditional end to the strike because there was nothing traditional about the strike itself. In most cases when public employees strike against their employer, one organization represents the employees,

FEA in this instance, and that representative negotiates against a single entity representing management. The Florida statewide walkout bore practically no resemblance to that norm. In order to resolve the strike, FEA had to deal directly or indirectly with multiple state jurisdictions: sixty-seven county school boards, two houses of the legislature, a governor, and a cabinet (not to mention organized opposition from Associated Industries and other nongovernmental groups).

To add to the enormity of FEA's task, because Florida had no collective bargaining statute there were no bargaining or conflict resolution procedures available to the parties. That meant, among other things, that each of the various governmental entities FEA faced could, and did, act independently of each other, and sometimes in contradiction to one another.

Then there was the matter of the resignations. As indicated earlier, teachers had, in writing, voluntarily unemployed themselves. Among other things, that meant that every county school board was free to make independent decisions about when and under what circumstance they would hire back striking teachers, if at all. The school boards were not restricted or constrained in that respect by any Florida law or agency. Consequently, some counties could choose to "forgive and forget," putting the whole episode behind them, while others could choose to impart significant retribution.

Those school boards that did choose to fire individual teachers or administrators often caused the strike to extend well beyond the initial three weeks in their counties because the rest of the county's teachers refused to return to work without them. Those school boards also had to contend with legal challenges from NEA, FEA, and local associations.

By allowing the bill to become law without his signature on March 7, 1968, Governor Kirk performed an extraordinary political pirouette. After stridently and repeatedly promising to veto the legislation produced by the special session of the legislature, he unexpectedly reversed course. By letting the bill become law absent his signature, Kirk accomplished two goals: first, he avoided the potential for widening the strike, and second, he also figured to save face with the voters by claiming that he hadn't technically approved a tax increase. When he ran for reelection in 1970, he could claim that he had kept his promise to the electorate not to increase taxes, and that it was the legislature that had caved in to FEA over his objections.

A few have speculated that Governor Kirk had planned that course of action all along. Perhaps. Whatever his motives or political gambits, however, it is clear that if Kirk had signed the special session's bill upon its passage in February, or even announced at the time of its passage that he would allow it to become law without his signature, FEA would have signed on, and there would never have been a teacher strike.

A few others have claimed that the reason Kirk did not veto the special session's bill was because he didn't have enough Republican support left in the legislature to sustain the veto. They speculate that if FEA had withheld striking and waited for the governor to either sign the bill or let it go into effect without his signature, it could have won the day without a strike.

The problem with that revisionist speculation is twofold: FEA had every reason to believe that Kirk would veto the special session's education bill because he had always followed through on his veto threats before, and, there was nothing whatsoever to indicate to FEA that Republican legislators would abandon Kirk for this particular veto. They had, after all, sustained his vetoes throughout the previous summer and fall. FEA would have been foolish to assume that Republican legislators would suddenly desert the governor they had consistently supported.

In any event, it was what it was, and Kirk did what he did. After all his bellicose name-calling, threats, and posturing, the governor publicly washed his hands of the whole affair—much like a modern day Pontius Pilate—and proclaimed that the onus for the settlement and resultant tax increase was on the hands of the legislature.

On March 8, the day after the legislation became law and just prior to FEA's announcing the end of the strike, the State Board of Education approved a nine-point settlement with FEA calling for an additional $10.2 million for education during the current school year. FEA accepted the settlement, which contained a provision urging school boards to reinstate all the striking teachers who had resigned to their former positions without reprisals. FEA then told its locals to return to work on Monday, March 11.

Because there were no procedures in place to get everyone back at the same time and under the same conditions, teachers in the various counties went back to work at different junctures. Twenty-seven school districts honored the no reprisals provision and fully reinstated all the teachers and administrators, but most local school boards blithely ignored it. Some went on vindictive rampages, hell bent to make their teachers and administrators pay dearly for their temerity. For those teachers and principals who found themselves in a local school board's crosshairs, their only hope for reemployment resided in legal efforts of FEA, NEA, and their local associations.

Phil Constans and other FEA leaders had no real choice but to end the strike at that point because there was nothing more to be gained, literally and figuratively. Not only was the legislature unlikely to come up with more money after having gone through months of turmoil in its fights with both FEA and the governor, but it had also become exceedingly difficult for FEA to sustain the number of teachers remaining out on strike. Some estimates are that 15,000 of the original 35,000 strikers had returned to work by the time of the settlement.

When it became apparent that some school boards were determined to get a pound of flesh, Constans made a last-minute appeal to all FEA locals to either stay out or go out again, invoking the pledge made earlier that "no one goes back until everyone goes back." But it was too late. Most locals had already begun the process of returning to work and told Constans that it would be virtually impossible to reverse the process. The toothpaste would not go back into the tube

Some FEA locals continued to strike for another three or four weeks before reaching an agreement to return to the classrooms. In those locals, conflict was centered on over 8,500 teachers or principals who had been fired, transferred, reduced in salary, or otherwise disciplined. In some instances the strike continued because the school boards would not rehire any of the building principals who had walked out.

In some districts, such as Duval County, the school board flatly refused to hire back any administrators who had joined the walkout. Some administrators were eventually rehired but reassigned or demoted. The board also selected about five hundred tenured teachers to be hired back only on an annual contract basis, a demotion of sorts. Also a lawsuit by the school board against the NAACP for keeping children out of school helped keep the fire in Duval stoked for a considerable period. At the end of the fifth week, almost all the Duval teachers were back at work, but at least seven of them were still out three months later.

In Pasco County, each individual school board member publicly produced a list of teachers they would not allow back in the county. In Gadsden County, at least two teachers were told to "Get out of the county." In Dixie and Bay Counties the school boards pledged that they would never, under any circumstances, hire back any of the striking teachers. In Hernando, the school board not only refused to rehire any walkout Hernando teacher, but striking teachers from any other county. They maintained that no-hire policy for years.[1]

In Escambia County, teachers stayed on strike for an additional three weeks after March 8 because the school board initially refused to hire back any of the administrators and some of the teachers. Because the strike continued, at the beginning of the sixth week the board secured individual injunctions against 1,100 Escambia teachers in an effort to force them back into the classrooms. After being urged by the administrators to go back without them, the teachers reluctantly did. Most of Escambia's principals were eventually hired back, but many were demoted. Likewise, some teachers never got their jobs back.

Pinellas County had big problems. The school board accepted the resignations of all 1,776 teachers who went on strike and proceeded to hire their replacements. When the strike finally ended after seven bitter weeks, every teacher who wanted to return to work had to reapply individually for a teaching position. About one hundred of those who walked out, most of whom were experienced teachers at the top of the salary schedule, chose to leave the district rather than reapply. Many principals were fired, reassigned, or demoted. The Pinellas County Teachers Association members stuck together through it all, largely because of the leadership of their executive secretary, Larry Black.

In Broward County, the teachers had gone on strike over salaries a year earlier in 1967 and, as part of the settlement, agreed not to go out again if FEA should call a statewide strike. Even so, when FEA did call the strike, about five hundred Broward teachers went out with their striking colleagues. All of them returned to their classrooms at the end of the first week except for seventy-four Broward teachers who felt compelled to continue their walkout. Led by BCTA's president Marge Head, those seventy-four teachers were not only fired when the strike ended, but the Broward Board of Education successfully petitioned the state to have their Florida teaching licenses revoked. They became known as the "Broward 74."

In Dade County, the president, vice president, and executive secretary were held in contempt of court. The local was fined $30,000 and Pat Tornillo was sentenced to two years in jail (which he never had to serve). Because of its size and strength its members fared fairly well when the strike ended. In fact, during the strike, Tornillo had cut a deal with the Dade superintendent that once the strike was over, all Dade teachers would go back to their jobs without retribution.

And so it went from county to county. Three weeks after the strike ended, thousands of Florida's striking teachers were still unemployed, including NEA's president Braulio Alonzo, a Hillsborough County principal. Both FEA and NEA worked with local associations in a variety of ways, including lawsuits, to get many fired teachers restored to their former positions, but it took more than a year for the dust to settle from all the rehiring, transfers, demotions, fines, lawsuits, and the like. By 1970 most of the striking teachers who still wanted to return were reemployed in their old school districts.

While all the debris from the strike eventually settled, the psychological trauma experienced by many of the teachers was deeply felt for many years to come. Much of that trauma, although muted, still remains forty years later.

8

LOOKING BACK A DAY LATER

Examining the aftermath of the 1968 teacher strike in Florida is like watching a comet traverse the sky. Most of what you see is not the comet itself, but the trail of debris that follows it. So it is with the 1968 strike. Repercussions from the walkout were brilliant in the sky for almost two decades afterward, and on a clear night traces of the tail are still visible. The strike delivered dramatic results for teachers, consequential results for the State of Florida, a political ending for Claude Kirk Jr., and a crippling fallout for the Florida Education Association.

On the plus side for education, the walkout produced some very practical results that could be considered victories. The money appropriated for education during the special session was more than had ever been generated before in any preceding session of the legislature. The package approved by the legislature and enacted into law without Kirk's signature allocated about $250 million in new spending, with about $175 million earmarked for K–12 education. That meant over $2,000 for every classroom in the state.

It was the largest education appropriation ever, but, unfortunately at the time, the precise amount became a back-and-forth dispute between FEA and the legislature. FEA originally took the position that the package allocated something less than $150 million actually going to the public schools, but later revised its estimate upward.

Regardless of the haggling over exact numbers, the bottom line was that there were substantially more funds for Florida's public schools than there ever would have been without all the fuss. It was the largest financial injection the schools had ever received in the history of the state, and the salary increases teachers received were also the highest they had ever received. Florida salaries went from twenty-second in the nation the year of the strike to thirteenth the following year. They had never ranked that high before and haven't since.

Some critics have said that the strike was unnecessary because the amount of money in the package when the walkout ended was the same amount that was on the table at its beginning. A shallow case can be made to support this contention, but to accept it at face value once again engages in revisionist history. It also allows Florida's power structure to obviate FEA's success, and lets itself off the hook for abandoning education and forcing teachers out of their classrooms.

In the first place, the legislature would never have put the kind of money that it did into the final budget settlement without the real threat of a looming statewide strike. It was the pressure applied by FEA that forced the special session of the legislature and ultimately produced significant additional funding. The legislature's pathetic record of education funding and counterfeit promises over the previous two decades ratifies that point dramatically. In other words, without the special session and the strike, the low tax obsession would have continued its omnipotent reign unabated.

The second reason why the funds would never have been forthcoming without the strike was that when the special session adjourned, Governor Kirk publicly vowed to veto the bill just as he had done many times before. If FEA had not gone out, and if Kirk had indeed vetoed the bill, there is no doubt that the old scenario of no new money for education would have once again prevailed. Further, FEA would have been rendered a paper tiger in the eyes of the power structure, the media, and its own membership.

Of course, the whole premise of the argument that the strike was all about teacher salaries is deceptive. The strike was *not* only about teachers' salaries. Most of those who walked off their jobs did so because they wanted the state to do something positive about the deplorable state of educational neglect.

While it is most assuredly true that teachers were upset about their poor pay, according to those who went out, at least two other factors were more important. First, the teachers were alarmed by, and fed up with, the constant deterioration of the state's education programs. FEA and the teachers made that point over and over again before and during the walkout. It was the primary reason why they conducted the Crisis Sunday effort to get citizens to come to the schools to observe and discuss these issues.

Year after frustrating year, they had pleaded with state and county governments to do something about special education programs, to make sure that every county provided kindergartens, to improve the embarrassing lack of school supplies, to get new textbooks to replace the tattered and obsolete ones in use, to repair and maintain dilapidated buildings, to be able to attract and retain qualified teachers, and on and on. None of those concerns were addressed.

Another reason that it is simplistic to attribute the strike solely to teacher salaries is that it ignores the tremendous amount of frustration that had built up over the years within the teaching ranks over nonsalary issues. Teachers collectively believed that those responsible for public education in the State of Florida didn't really give a damn about them or the students they taught.

Promises had been made to educators year after year, only to be summarily abandoned without the slightest fear of consequence. Florida's teachers had come to believe that nothing was ever going to improve unless they did something about it in a way that politicians could not ignore. To Florida's teachers, the strike was both an act of rebellion against the indifference of the power structure and a demonstration of their own commitment to education.

Another important factor in the walkout was the behavior of Governor Claude Kirk Jr. While the teachers didn't go on strike because of Kirk by any means, they came to see him as the embodiment of their nemesis: the low tax, low public service culture of the state. He, more than any other politician, personified the rapacious, self-indulgent nature of Florida politics.

Kirk's high living and confrontational rhetoric about taxes, teachers, and teacher unions turned off teachers completely. While they were begging for textbooks, smaller classes, and supplies, he was running around the country in self-aggrandizing pursuit of his own agenda. His flamboyance and cavalier attitude toward FEA didn't help.

During the strike, the Florida power structure, strongly influenced by the antiunion industrial lobby, harped on two recurrent themes: that teachers were being selfish and unreasonable in demanding higher pay, and that FEA was nothing more than a power hungry union in pursuit of collective bargaining rights in Florida.

These accusations were grist for the power structure's propaganda mill, but they trivialized the reality that teachers had families, bills, and obligations that required the same legal tender as everyone else. They had to pay the same prices at the grocery store, the car dealership, and the doctor's office. There was nothing wrong then and there is nothing wrong now with teachers wanting to make a decent living as professionals.

The old bromide offered up repeatedly by the legislature—"There are only so many slices of the pie"—is a thinly disguised political metaphor to justify Florida's low tax obsession. It obviates even the perfunctory, let alone thoughtful, consideration of getting a bigger pie. Forty years ago, most of the editorialists, and all too many citizens, considered teachers public servants. They saw them as akin to monks and nuns who should be so devoted to public service that they willingly forsake material things like money. It is completely self-serving for the power structure to suggest that there is something inherently wrong about teachers resenting their depressed economic status.

In the most ironic twist of all, within a few years after the walkout FEA, through court challenges and legislative action, was able to achieve collective bargaining for public employees. It is incontrovertible that the strike had an impact on gaining a collective bargaining statute. For his entire term of office, Governor Kirk had demonized FEA by charging that all it was really after was collective bargaining and power, not education. He said, "We in Florida do not plan to turn education over to a union. It is un-American to turn education over to unions."[1]

It is certainly true that FEA's Dade and Pinellas locals in particular had been advocating for a public employee collective bargaining law for several years. However, Kirk's accusations were a red herring designed to divert attention away from the teachers' real concerns. The issue of collective bargaining for teachers was neither the cause of the strike nor the militancy leading up to it; the issue, stated over and over by FEA and NEA, was the deterioration of education in Florida. So how did collective bargaining come about within just a few years after the strike? Where did the power structure's determination to keep public sector unions powerless break down?

On September 18, 1968, the Florida Supreme Court ruled in *Dade County Classroom Teachers Association v. Ryan* that state law did not prohibit public employees, including teachers, from bargaining collectively, and that they did, in fact, have collective bargaining rights. At the same time, however, the court also reaffirmed that public employees did not have the right to strike. This was, of course, a sweet victory for FEA and the educators of Florida, especially since local school boards and state legislators had been asserting for years that collective bargaining for teachers was unconstitutional. Without question, the court decision was an indirect outgrowth of the statewide walkout.

All that remained for collective bargaining to become a reality was for the legislature to draft the appropriate legislation to set the parameters and procedures. That was easier said than done, however, because of the staunch opposition of Governor Kirk and the antiunion, antitax lobby. The Associated Industries of Florida, Florida League of Cities, Florida School Boards Association, and Florida Association of County Commissioners all combined forces to argue that public sector collective bargaining would increase the cost of government, which in turn would increase taxes.[2]

Things began to change when a new governor, Reubin Askew, a Democrat and proponent of collective bargaining, was elected to office in 1970. In 1974 the Florida legislature was faced with the Supreme Court's threat to write the procedures and rules itself if the legislature didn't enact a statute and rules. The legislature then passed the statute establishing procedures for collective bargaining for public employees. This win came after years of an uphill struggle by FEA, its urban locals, the state's firefighters, AFSCME, AFL-CIO, and other progressive organizations, but it was clearly FEA's victory.

Through all the fog of war and the lapses of memory brought on by the passage of time, one dynamic of the 1968 teacher walkout comes through over and over again. FEA demonstrated true, albeit naive, grit when it decided to take on Florida's inbred economic culture. FEA leaders and members marched headlong into battle with both trepidation and conviction. They believed what Phil Constans had said to them in the Tangerine Bowl the previous summer: "If the teaching profession must die in Florida, let it be with dignity, with courage, and with integrity. For it is truly better to 'die on your feet than to live on your knees.'"[3] The teachers (or at least half of them) responded with a firm "Amen."

9

FALLOUT AT FEA

The 1968 walkout unleashed a tempest of repercussions in all directions and at all levels, and the aftermath lasted for years. No one escaped it. The Florida Education Association and its locals suffered through the storm's fury amid internal political turmoil. Some individual teachers suffered by being subjected to recriminations and firings by some school boards. Many school boards endured spasms of lawsuits and conflicts with FEA and its locals. Governor Kirk lost his reelection bid.

Following the walkout, FEA experienced a good deal of consternation within its ranks over what direction the organization should take for the future. There were many reasons for angst within the FEA's body politic, not the least of which was that in 1969, the year after the strike, FEA experienced a significant drop-off in membership, falling from almost 50,000 members to 22,000. Somewhere between half and two-thirds of that loss was due to fact that the huge Dade, Hillsborough, and Pinellas locals pulled out of FEA and went independent.

Of course, there was an abundance of Monday morning quarterbacking over the strike strategies and tactics that had been employed by FEA. There were also repercussions from some quarters over the uneven and sometimes chaotic way the strike had ended. Questions arose about whether or not FEA should have turned in the resignations, and about its inability to negotiate a statewide settlement that protected all the striking teachers.

As is the case after every traumatic confrontation, there was an abundance of finger pointing and second-guessing within FEA and its locals about practically everything. The only thing virtually everyone agreed on was the need to have done something dramatic to challenge the educational status quo.

By far, however, the most overriding and overarching questions centered on the future direction of the organization. One school of thought was that FEA should disavow its adventure into militancy and return to its nonconfrontational, nonunion, professional way of life. But, by far the prevailing sentiment was to go in the opposite direction: to become a real union and pursue a state collective bargaining law. Achieving that objective would mean that FEA locals would bargain for its members against their school boards under the auspices of a state statute.

There was a third direction advocated by some within the leadership of FEA, and that was to just rest awhile, take stock, and take time to cogitate about the future. The people in this camp stood little chance of prevailing because poststrike events and circumstances were flying fast and furious, and organizational somnolence was therefore reduced to the status of a fantasy. There were also strong and mounting pressures from urban locals to change the organization's structure and policies. All in all, the poststrike state of FEA was unsettled, to say the least.

One of the circumstances that prevented FEA from resting on its oars was the incursion of the American Federation of Teachers (AFT), its organizational rival, into Florida. Because of the turmoil resulting from the strike, AFT had been presented with an opportunity to unfurl its union flag in Florida. Consequently, AFT organizers arrived in the Sunshine State to sign up new members and establish new local unions.

Over the next several years, AFT enjoyed early organizing success— partially because of its organizing and partly because of local mergers in Dade, Duval, Suwannee, and higher education—that touched off protracted organizational warfare in Florida between NEA and AFT.

In April 1969, FEA fired Phil Constans. He had been a cutting edge and inspirational leader, but he also had detractors on the FEA board who thought he was radioactive coming off the walkout. Of course, quite a few leaders were simply looking for a scapegoat.

The National Education Association, for its part, thought Constans had gone too far too fast in promoting the strike and had made serious errors of judgment. This was true even in spite of the fact that NEA's on-site emissary to FEA, Cecil Hannan, had collaborated with Constans every step of the way. Many on the FEA board desired to ease back on the polarization that had taken place between FEA and the legislature, and felt that animus toward FEA was likely to continue if Constans remained.

The board replaced Constans with Wally Johnson, a staff member from NEA's Washington State affiliate, who was more compatible with the conservative elements on the board. However, if the FEA board of directors thought Constans's firing and Johnson's hiring would bring internal tranquility, it was in for a major disappointment; FEA found itself standing on a political hill of sand.

The sand was shifting because while large segments of FEA's leadership, including the board of directors, were neither union oriented nor militant, FEA members, especially their local leaders, increasingly were. The activists in the organization pushed FEA toward a more aggressive teacher advocacy agenda.

Acceding to pressures from its urban locals to get more local representation in the state association's policy-making apparatus, FEA agreed to the creation of a "structure committee" for the purpose of generating recommendations for changes in the organization's structure. In 1970, the second year of its operation, the committee, chaired by Jim Geiger, president of the Pasco County local and one of the young Turks within FEA, succeeded in getting several of its recommendations adopted by the 1970 FEA Delegate Assembly. At that assembly, Ken Etterman from Sarasota, running on the platform espoused by the Structure Committee, was elected FEA president.[1]

Of paramount importance among FEA's new policies had been a provision for the unification of membership at the local, state, and national level. That meant that, for the first time, when teachers joined the organization at the local level, they also had to join the other two levels (state and national). Largely because of this new policy, three of FEA's largest locals, Dade, Pinellas, and Hillsborough, known as "the big three," went independent—meaning they had no state or national affiliation. They were now outside FEA's firmament.

Also enacted by the delegate assembly were provisions that general services to members were to be provided at the local level, with only specialized services provided by the state and/or national organizations. Dues were to be apportioned between the three levels based upon the services provided. Also, there was to be a more direct governance link between leaders at the local, state, and national organizations. Some of the new policies were to be implemented by July 1, 1972.

Many of the recommendations of the structure committee, including those approved and adopted by the Delegate Assembly, were anathema to Johnson and the board of directors. Of primary concern to them was the shift in organizational power from the state association to the locals, along with the redistribution of dues in that direction. As a result of their opposition to the new policies, FEA leaders dragged their collective feet in adopting the committee's recommendations.

As the debate about direction and philosophy at the state level raged on, FEA's local associations were all over the map in terms of their own future plans. They essentially broke down into three groups: (1) Those locals that wanted to retain affiliation with FEA and NEA and seek change from within the organization; (2) those locals that wanted to leave FEA and affiliate with AFT, believing that the most effective way toward collective bargaining and militancy was through AFT and organized labor (AFL-CIO); and (3) those locals that believed they could be more effective on their own as independents, unaffiliated with any state or national organization.

With FEA's future direction at sixes and sevens, a cadre of assertive, visionary leaders emerged who sought to put it all back together. They desired to provide FEA with a new direction and a structure more responsive to local needs, which meant getting more urban leaders into state policy making positions. They also strongly desired to bring all Florida teachers and their locals back into one state organization.

The latter goal ultimately proved to be the most difficult by far to achieve, particularly since many on the FEA board were not really interested in getting the Dade, Pinellas, and Hillsborough locals back in the fold. The prevailing attitude on the board seemed to be "let them go their own way." The board no doubt believed that life within FEA would be a lot less hectic without the disruption caused by those locals and their leaders: Pat Tornillo in Dade, Larry Black in Pinellas, and Bob Martinez in Hillsborough. All this internal disharmony stood in stark and ominous contrast to the unity FEA had experienced at the beginning of the walkout just a year or two earlier.

Much to the chagrin of the structure committee and its supporters, Johnson and the FEA board of directors continued to stall the implementation of the changes that had already been adopted by the 1970 Delegate Assembly. This was especially true of those policies related to providing more services to local associations and giving local leaders representation on the board. Frustration with FEA's inaction caused a group of local leaders within FEA to coalesce and take on the political task of forcing Johnson and the FEA board to restructure the organization's governance.

This group ultimately came to be called "New Direction" and worked to compel implementation of the changes adopted by the 1970 Delegate

Assembly. During the 1971–1972 year, Johnson not only resisted the direction of FEA president Ken Etterman, who favored the reforms, but he also challenged the reformers directly, relying on his comfortable margin of support on the FEA board.

After a series of confrontations between the reformers and the FEA policy makers over these and other issues, in 1972 the reformers were vindicated when the Delegate Assembly voted overwhelmingly to get rid of Johnson and have local leaders represented on the FEA board of directors.

The reformers had won the day. The board of directors was reconstituted and the new board wasted little time in heading in New Direction's new direction. After disengaging from Wally Johnson, in late 1972 the board hired Richard Batchelder, or "Batch" as he is known, as its new FEA executive secretary. Batchelder was from Massachusetts and in 1966 had served as NEA president; he had also served as executive director of the southern section of the California Teachers Association.

Upon assuming his new Florida post, Batch inherited a fragmented organization. Just over a year later in early 1974, Pat Tornillo led the Dade County Classroom Teacher Association and its 10,000 members into a local merger with the one hundred member AFT unit, the Dade Federation of Teachers. In the spring of that same year, the Duval Teachers Association successfully merged with the Jacksonville Federation of Teachers.

During this period, Batchelder, Tornillo, Cathy Luther (Duval and FEA president), and John Spriggs (Palm Beach and FEA president), along with several other FEA leaders, developed a merger plan to bring all the factions in Florida back together under one, much larger, roof. The plan was to make FEA an all-inclusive organization comprised of former AFT, NEA, and independent locals. It was to be called United Teachers of Florida, which later became FEA/United when NEA disaffiliated FEA. According to the blueprint, FEA/United and its locals would affiliate with both national organizations, NEA and AFT. For its part, FEA/United would also affiliate with AFL-CIO. It was a grand vision, but it was a flawed plan.

The insurmountable stumbling block to the merger was that NEA would not recognize the new state affiliate because, among other things, FEA/United would become an affiliate of AFL-CIO, a real no-no for NEA at that time. NEA made it clear to FEA/United that if the merger was consummated, it would disaffiliate FEA/United from NEA.

This rather myopic stand by NEA was largely the result of a trauma it had experienced a year or two earlier involving a similar state merger in New York between the NEA and AFT New York state affiliates. In that instance, after a rocky start, the new, merged state association disaffiliated from NEA and went over entirely to AFT. As a result, NEA ended up losing about 100,000 members in the State of New York almost overnight.

Despite NEA's dire warnings, FEA/United consummated the merger. It did so riding the wings of several assumptions (perhaps they were more like hopes). First, the FEA leaders were much more focused on their vision of bringing all Florida school employees together within the House of Labor than complying with an arcane by-law requirement of the National Education Association.

Consequently, FEA/U leaders hoped that NEA would come to see the shortsightedness of its position and join them in their quest for solidarity. In addition to their hopes that NEA would come around, FEA/United leaders could not bring themselves to believe that NEA would disaffiliate, or cut loose, more than 60,000 potential members in Florida—especially after having lost 100,000 in New York.

Without question, FEA/United's desire to affiliate with AFL-CIO was rooted in FEA's failure during the 1968 walkout to close down all Florida schools. Many came to believe that all school personnel, including secretaries, bus drivers, custodians, and others, needed to be unified under one banner. They also felt strongly that those delivering supplies to schools should support a strike; and that, so the thinking went, meant affiliation with AFL-CIO.

NEA followed through on its threat, and in 1974 did, indeed, disaffiliate the entire FEA/United state organization. NEA thereupon immediately set about organizing and chartering a brand new state affiliate in Florida. It dispatched organizers to the state in an effort to retain as many former FEA locals as possible under a new NEA state umbrella. In setting up the new state affiliate, NEA was hampered by the fact that for legal reasons, it could not use its old affiliate's name, Florida Education Association, and had to come up with a new appellation.

Arriving at a new name proved to be an issue. The early Florida leaders of the new NEA state affiliate, in a moment of either temporary insanity or severely retarded imagination, decided to name the new Florida NEA affiliate the *Florida United Services Organization* (FUSA), a non sequitur of a name that meant nothing to anyone, including its own members. A year later, in an almost undetectable spike of imagination, the FUSA Representative Assembly changed the organization's name to the Florida Teaching Profession (FTP).

Finally, in 1977 the delegates to the annual R.A. agreed to add NEA to the name, calling it the Florida Teaching Profession–National Education

Association, or FTP–NEA for short. This latest iteration of the organization's name provided at least some degree of recognition for the legislators and public.

FTP–NEA's first president was Carl Harner from Highlands County, and its first executive secretary was George Auzenne, a former Michigan staffer. With the founding of these two new organizations, in 1974 FEA/United and FTP–NEA dropped the starting flag on a twenty-six-year organizational race to the finish line. Taking stock ten years later, FEA/United had about half the Florida counties in its camp, including Dade, Duval, Alachua, and Sarasota, with a total membership of about 25,000. FTP–NEA had the other half of the counties in its camp, including Pinellas, Broward, Escambia, Palm Beach, and Orange, with a membership of about 25,000.

For years to come the two rival organizations flailed away at each other with relentless exuberance but with only occasional successes one way or the other. FTP–NEA gained considerable momentum when it became an early supporter of state senator Bob Graham in his quest for the governorship in 1978 against six other opponents, including the one endorsed by FEA/United. For almost three decades the membership of the two rivals continued to be split about evenly.

As the rivalry continued all the way to the twenty-first century, the membership totals in each organization grew to 40,000 or more. It was clearly a stalemate. Finally in the year 2000 the two state affiliates (and all Florida locals) merged into the present-day FEA. The twenty-six-year circle instigated by the 1968 state-wide walkout had finally been completed.

There were several reasons why the Florida merger succeeded in 2000 after it had gone down in flames twenty-six years earlier. For one thing, at the national level, NEA and AFT decided to stop fighting each other and work together. For another, both organizations had grown weary of the fight. They were resentful of the amount of money being wasted attacking each other, and they both faced common enemies and problems. Of no less importance, NEA had modified its opposition to affiliation with AFL-CIO. Times had changed, leaders had changed, and so had the attitudes of many NEA members about unionism.

In fact, in 1994 the leadership of the two national organizations, the National Education Association (NEA), and the American Federation of Teachers (AFT) began formal merger discussions at the national level. AFT, under the leadership of Al Shanker (president), Ed McElroy (treasurer), and Sandy Feldman (vice president, and president after Shanker's death) stepped up to the plate. So did NEA's leaders including Keith Geiger (president),

Bob Chase (vice president and the president succeeding Geiger), and Don Cameron, executive director). Although NEA's Representative Assembly turned down a tentative merger agreement in New Orleans in 1998, trust levels between the two organizations had grown significantly and the raiding of locals between the two organizations had all but evaporated.

Given those circumstances, the leaders of Florida's two rivals, FEA/United and FTP–NEA, demonstrated history-making courage and vision by not only commencing merger discussions, but also bringing them to fruition. And, they did it the right way, in complete cooperation with the two national organizations. After three decades of all-out war, Florida's organizational shards were glued back together by the hands of visionary state organizational leadership.

Those who brought the bacon home for the two Florida organizations from FEA/United were Andy Ford (president in Duval), Pat Tornillo (FEA/United president), Jack Carbone (FEA/United staff) and Bob Lee (FEA/United treasurer). FTP–NEA can largely thank Aaron Wallace (president in the early stages), Jeff Wright (staffer and former president), Maureen Dinnen (president when the merger took place), and John Ryor (executive director).

It is, of course, self-evident at both the national level and in Florida that there were other key, even pivotal, players in the merger efforts that are not mentioned here. Some of those leaders labored beneath the radar screen, and others served on the negotiating teams.

Today FEA is Florida's largest union and is affiliated nationally with both NEA and AFT. Interestingly, it is one of the largest state affiliates in each of those two national organizations. That distinction is especially meaningful and ironic given the history of the internecine thirty-year war in Florida between NEA and AFT. The thirty-year organizational warfare in Florida and the ultimate merger that put it all back together are directly descended from, and attributable to, the 1968 walkout.

10

FALLOUT AT NEA

The National Education Association was a reluctant but critical participant in the 1968 Florida statewide strike. There is no other way to put
it. The principle reason for its reluctance to become engaged was exactly
the same reason that FEA was conflicted about its own mission in 1968: the
old guard was still in control of the organization even as the young Turks
and urban locals within the organization were agitating for change. When
the statewide walkout in Florida occurred, not only had NEA yet to resolve
its own internal politics regarding whether it should be a union or professional association, but it caught NEA without sufficient personnel on staff
who were experienced in bargaining and organizing. Neither did it have
the necessary financial resources required. The bottom line, however, was
that NEA had little choice but to support fully its Florida state affiliate, and
that's what it did.

In 1968 NEA was going through a gut-wrenching internal political
battle between those who advocated a more militant organization dedicated
to collective bargaining, unionism, and strikes if necessary, and those who
wanted to retain the established professional policies and the image it had
worked for over a century to cultivate. The profound organizational
changes that NEA experienced during this period would have literally
caused most organizations to founder. All the while this transitional change
was occurring, NEA had to continue providing services to its affiliates and
members who were themselves in various stages of transition. What was
going on in Florida was just one manifestation of similar activities taking
place all over the country.

For several years prior to the Florida walkout, younger, more assertive,
local and state leaders had been forcing NEA's old guard to give up its hold

on the organization, and the NEA hierarchy was, indeed, rapidly losing its grip on power. The militant wing of NEA, led by its urban affiliates through an organization called the National Council of Urban Education Associations (NCUEA), was clearly on the ascendancy and on the verge of takeover. Florida urban locals, including Dade, Duval, Pinellas, and Hillsborough, were a key part of the urban surge within NEA. Pat Tornillo and Janet Dean from Dade County were key players. Within just a few years at the end of the 1960s and into the early 1970s, NEA morphed into a full-bodied, full-throated, union, albeit unaffiliated with organized labor.

But unionism wasn't the only transitional change taking place within NEA when the Florida strike came along. At about the same time, the organization was waving goodbye to the various administrator groups that had always been part of its structure. The old NEA Department of Classroom Teachers became, in essence, the entire organization. Not only that, but the merger of the previously segregated black and white NEA state affiliates took place in 1966, and that melding also required a great deal of time and effort. Then, too, NEA was deeply involved in the civil rights and women's rights movements. To be sure, in 1968 NEA had a load on its back, and the last thing it needed or wanted was a prolonged statewide strike in Florida or anywhere else.

In June 1967 NEA applied sanctions on the state of Florida, but before doing so had sent a high-powered team of college professors and representatives from other education organizations to conduct an investigation of the entire Florida education system. Its report, which was thorough, critical, and powerful in its impact, had an electrifying effect on the Florida power structure as it set the stage for the sanctions. After receiving the report and issuing several warnings to Florida's governor and legislature, NEA did, in fact, apply sanctions.

When it came to the Florida strike, in order to provide resources to Florida that it didn't immediately possess, NEA got creative. For example, because NEA only employed a handful of organizers, it sent out a clarion call to its collective bargaining state affiliates to send experienced bargaining and organizing staff to Florida. The states responded by sending between fifty and seventy-five staffers to the state during the strike. These staffers came mostly from collective bargaining states such as Michigan, Connecticut, Massachusetts, and New York, and proved to be of invaluable assistance to FEA's striking locals.

In addition, NEA spent about $2.5 million to provide grants and loans to striking FEA members, most of which it had to borrow. Many of the members who went out in Florida say that they could not have made it if it were not for the biweekly checks they received from NEA. NEA also provided lawyers and legal assistance to both FEA and its members. One of NEA's top executives (from the union side of the organization), Cecil Hannan, spent months in Florida working directly with Phil Constans and FEA leadership. He also interacted with the governor's office, politicians, and local associations. He was NEA's eyes and ears in Florida. His assistant, Larry Sorensen, another organizer, provided logistical and strategic assistance for the same period of time.

Many at NEA credit its assistant executive secretary, Allan West, for providing the impetus and support Florida needed, as well as being the shepherd for the militant side of NEA's split organizational personality at the time. That kind of direction certainly did not emanate from the office of the NEA's top administrator, executive secretary Sam Lambert. Lambert was trepidatious at best, and at worst opposed to the whole Florida venture (he was not alone within NEA's hierarchy). However, in a speech to the NEA Representative Assembly in July 1968, in describing the Florida effort, Lambert said, "We reversed a ten-year trend of educational neglect and decay." He also said, "We increased the financial outlays for education by at least $2,000 per classroom."[1] His enthusiasm for the results of the strike belied his personal opposition to it. Before he was fired in 1972, Lambert had publicly criticized the Florida walkout.

The bottom line is that NEA came through with the necessary support that FEA required. Today, of course, there would be no controversy about supporting a state or local affiliate on strike. One must remember, however that NEA did not change its policy opposing strikes until its Representative Assembly in July 1968—after the Florida strike was already over. Given all of that, NEA's support for FEA and the strike was really quite remarkable. NEA provided the assistance by being creative and dealing with its internal conflicts privately. It was like building an airplane while flying it.

11

LOOKING BACK
FORTY YEARS LATER

Over the last forty years there has been a great deal of introspection and analysis as to how the strike could have been avoided. Without question it could have been. Although the walkout was what it was, when it is viewed from the vantage point of four decades past, it is clear that different decisions by either the legislature, Governor Kirk, or FEA might well have produced a less confrontational result.

In many ways, the Florida strike was a perfect political storm. At least six volatile and implacable storm elements conspired to send the state into turmoil. The first of these elements was (and is) the state's dysfunctional obsession with low taxes. The second factor was the political and social turmoil gripping the country; taking to the streets had become a legitimate vehicle for protesting. Third was the string of legislative sessions in the 1960s that refused to acknowledge the state's deteriorating education system, let alone address it. Fourth on the list was a governor so enthralled with confrontation and publicity that he was more interested in the fight than the solution. Fifth was the immense buildup of frustration among the state's teachers. The last element that produced the perfect storm was the strategic decisions made by FEA.

Each of these factors was critical, but no single element alone was enough to produce what happened. When they all came together, however, they presented an insurmountable force. Although forty years of lapsed time has dulled the sense of angst and frustration experienced by the parties involved, in some respects the picture of what they faced and did has become clearer.

THE LOW TAX FLORIDA MENTALITY

As noted many times, Florida is a state that has always been obsessed with low taxation, and it is no less true today. That obsession was built into Florida's governmental system and political culture at the state's inception and its grip has been sustained for more than one hundred years. If it were not for the large number of tourists streaming across Florida's borders from all over America and Europe, particularly since World War II, its economy would never have survived the government's low tax operations.

THE LEGISLATURE

Especially during the years leading up to the perfect storm, the Florida legislature, which is charged by the state constitution to provide a quality education system for all students, fell asleep at the wheel. Session after session of the legislature proudly hoisted its "keep taxes low" pennant to the top of the mast. For generations, Florida's elected officials had dedicated themselves to promoting private enterprise at the expense of public services.

Because Florida's legislatures were historically malapportioned, the state ceded its power to rural and industrial special interests, all but ignoring its population centers in the process. Only in the 1960s when the Supreme Court mandated reapportionment based on a one person–one vote principal did the state reluctantly begin to change.

As far as the state power structure was concerned, education was a commodity to be acquired on the cheap and teachers were viewed as indentured servants. When successive legislatures in the early and mid 1960s refused to do anything to stop the disgraceful deterioration of Florida's public schools, when they refused to listen to the pleas of the state's educators, and when they rededicated themselves to worshiping the low tax gods, they played their part in creating the perfect storm.

GOVERNOR CLAUDE KIRK JR.

As far as education generally, and the teacher strike in particular, is concerned, Claude Kirk Jr. was the wrong governor at the wrong time with the wrong priorities. With education deteriorating and frustrated teachers rapidly losing hope, the last thing the situation needed was a governor dedicated to confrontation and grandstanding. Unfortunately, that's what the State of Florida and the Florida Education Association got when Kirk was elected.

Many people to this day believe that Kirk actually orchestrated the confrontation with FEA in order to make political hay by taking on "a union determined to achieve collective bargaining" as he liked to say. While Claude Kirk did not single-handedly cause the statewide strike, it is no less true that he relished the confrontation and did virtually nothing to avoid it.

Kirk's arrogant and unilateral line item vetoes of the 1967 legislature's education budget turned a bad situation into a disastrous one. Coupled with his bellicose taunting of FEA, Kirk's education appropriation vetoes deliberately fanned a smoldering fire and caused FEA to distrust him. His election promise to make Florida's education first in the nation proved to be not only hollow, but—as far as educators were concerned—duplicitous as well.

Kirk had promoted himself as a problem-solver for education, but was actually a problem-maker. He did very little to improve education in the state, and when he left office virtually all the state's education's problems that he inherited were still in existence. The strike was a public relations disaster for the governor and caused his political star to dim immeasurably. By being in California when the strike began, and by threatening to veto the special session's education package, Floridians began to see him for the showman that he was instead of an education reformer.

In fact, almost as many Floridians blamed Governor Kirk for the walk-out as they did FEA. Everywhere he went during the strike angry crowds met him. His correspondence, while not wholly negative, was at least as critical as supportive of his handling of the crisis. His public approval ratings slipped. The education issue and the strike inflicted lasting damage on Kirk. He also lost much of his Republican support.

THE FLORIDA EDUCATION ASSOCIATION

To this day FEA strike leaders consider the strike a modest success in terms of bringing Florida's educational woes out into the open and forcing the state to come up with substantially more money for education. Much more significantly, the teachers who went out still feel a sense of pride in that effort. Nevertheless, almost all FEA leaders past and present agree that FEA made some serious errors in managing the strike. Many feel that given those errors, FEA was lucky to have come out of the strike as well as it did.

In retrospect, the single biggest mistake made by FEA was adopting the strategy of having the teachers resign from their jobs. The concept originally centered on the notion that since strikes were illegal, if there was no employment relationship between the teachers and their school boards, they couldn't be punished or ordered back to work. In an ideal world, and in a perfect scenario, such a scheme could have worked.

The strategy, however, depended almost entirely on closing down most, if not all, the state's schools, and having all the strike participants act in unison. The idea of closing the schools and keeping them closed until a settlement with the legislature was affected—and with the teachers immune from punishment because of the resignations—had a certain extraordinary logic to it.

The high-risk strategy backfired to an appreciable degree because FEA did not close down all the schools, and because only half the state's teachers walked out. The defections that occurred during the walkout also wounded FEA severely. So did the hiring of replacements to keep schools operating.

In any event, by allowing each county school board to decide who would be rehired and who wouldn't, and deciding which striking teachers would be punished and which wouldn't, FEA lost a great deal of leverage in getting all the strikers back to work. Neither had FEA prepared for the vindictiveness of some of the school boards.

In retrospect, FEA might have been better off to orchestrate having two or three different counties around the state strike, without resigning, at different times during the school year. While much more difficult to choreograph, such a strategy might have offered a better chance to protect the strikers' jobs. On the other hand, it surely would have produced countermeasures by the governor and the school boards.

Another alternative strategy could have been to simply call the statewide strike without resignations and let the chips fall where they may. FEA rejected this approach largely because it believed that most Florida teachers, given their antiunion inclinations, would never "strike" per se despite their demands for action.[1] We will never know whether that assumption was accurate, but given the teachers later rapid conversion to unionism and collective bargaining, the assumption was at least worth testing. On the other hand, some veterans of the walkout still, to this day, refuse to call it a strike.

THE TEACHERS

For the teachers who participated in the walkout, there is only one way to ascertain whether or not they thought the experience was worth it, and that's to ask those who are still around. It's not difficult to get answers, because for them (almost all of whom have retired long ago) it's like the walk-out occurred yesterday. For them time was, indeed, captured in a bottle.

Strike veterans recount events, dates, names, incidents, and feelings with amazing clarity and sometimes startling emotions. Teachers reminisce about friendships made and broken, marriages rent asunder, the animus exhibited by some local citizens, the mean-spiritedness of their school boards, and resentment at the actions of much of the business community.

Some views and feelings expressed by the participants are virtually unanimous. For example, during interviews with strike participants, whenever Governor Claude Kirk's name comes up—as it inevitably does—eyes roll with the same degree of disbelief, bemusement, and anger as ever. Many offered the unsolicited observation that the governor was commonly referred to as "Kirk the Jerk." When scouring their memories, some teachers got angry all over again. Some wept.

Not unlike World War II veterans, some of the former strike participants found it very difficult to start talking about their experience, but then, once started, couldn't stop. Memories cascade down, one upon the other, in a torrent of remembrances. The picture they paint today is not discolored by the passage of time, and the clarity of their original purpose is still sharp in their minds. With rare exceptions, no matter what happened to them personally, they still believe the strike was worth it. Almost all express no regrets for having participated in the walkout, although most said they would not want to go through it again.

A common refrain heard from these veterans goes along these lines: "We had to do something dramatic because the legislature and governor weren't doing right by the kids and they refused to listen." Another frequent comment is, "I feel proud that we stood together." A few strikers say, "Our salaries were so bad that we had to do something." There is a clear sense that they were fed up with the patronization and arrogance displayed by those in charge, and took great pride in telling the power structure to go to hell.

They demonstrated to the power structure that they were neither state chattel nor powerless drones. To almost all of them, it really doesn't matter whether the public or the politicians believe they won or lost the strike. They feel strongly that they did what they had to do; they brought the issues of education neglect to the front pages. They know full well that they and FEA lost the public relations battle. With a few notable exceptions, like the St. Petersburg Times, the media lined up behind the legislature and school boards. From the teachers' perspective, however, the conditions of the schools, the absence of teacher resources, the lack of proper education funding, and the shortcomings of the curricula were hung out for all to see.

The package finally approved by the legislature and allowed to become law without the governor's signature provided more money for education than ever before in the history of the state. After all the conflict, name-calling, and recriminations, the legislature and the governor did raise taxes, albeit grudgingly and spitefully. The low tax obsession of the state took a minor but important hit.

It is no less than sardonic that the very same school boards that had vilified and punished their teachers for having the temerity to go on strike gladly and unabashedly scooped up the increased funding that resulted from their effort. Not a single school board refused to take the additional funds that came their way. It's no less hypocritical that teachers who refused to strike because of their principles nevertheless accepted their otherwise nonexistent pay increases without a second thought.

The strike produced some immediate gains for FEA and its members, although other tangential benefits came a little later. It is sheer poetic justice that after all Governor Kirk's denunciations of teacher unions and collective bargaining, and after Associated Industries' fierce determination to keep unionism out of the public employee arena, in 1974 the state legislature passed a public employee collective bargaining statute for the state of Florida.

Many of the characters involved in the strike went on to better (or worse) fates. Governor Claude Kirk served only one term in office. He was defeated in his bid for reelection in 1972 even though many of his political positions and decisions had been taken with one eye on getting reelected. His promise of no new taxes got him into the Governor's Mansion, but his willingness to jettison the other half of his promise (to provide the best education system in the country) cost him dearly. Many Floridians considered him responsible for the statewide teachers' strike and resented him for it. Kirk was a candescent political meteor that raced across Florida's political skies and then disappeared into the night.

Commissioner of Education Floyd Christian, Governor Kirk's favorite whipping boy, and one of the few voices of moderation during the strike, left office in disgrace in 1974. He was indicted on nineteen counts of bribery, conspiracy, and perjury unrelated to the walkout or the education crisis.

Ralph Turlington, Speaker of the Florida House of Representatives, also tried to be a moderating force during his legislative days. He later succeeded Christian as Commissioner of Education and served in that capacity for fourteen years before retiring to live in North Carolina.

Pat Tornillo, who headed up the Dade county effort during the strike, continued to run the Dade union and FEA/United for thirty years before humiliating himself and the teachers he represented by using teachers' dues to feather his own nest. He was brought down in disgrace in 2002 after being indicted and sent to jail for squandering union money on personal interests. He died shortly after leaving prison in 2007. It has taken the Dade local, under the leadership of its current president Karen Aronowitz, along with FEA, AFT and NEA, several years and a great deal of hard work to rebuild both the union and its members' trust.

Bob Martinez, former Hillsborough CTA leader during the strike, went on to become Mayor of Tampa in 1986. Switching parties from Democrat to Republican, he ran for Governor in 1986 and was elected, becoming the second Republican Governor of Florida since reconstruction (following Claude Kirk). Interestingly, he was defeated for reelection by three time U.S. Senator Lawton Chiles, who had been a pro-education state senator during the walkout.

Braulio Alonso, a highly respected Hillsborough principal and NEA president at the time of the strike, was fired from his job in Tampa by the Hillsborough Board of Education. An intellectual and deeply religious man, Braulio had given many speeches around the state before and during the strike castigating the depressed status of Florida education. Claude Kirk publicly referred to him as "A rosary-carrying agent of Fidel Castro." After the strike, Alonzo accepted a staff position with NEA as its Director of International Relations before retiring several years later. He remains a prominent and revered Tampa citizen and has a high school named after him.

Phil Constans, FEA Executive Secretary during the strike, left FEA in 1969 and returned to teaching as a professor of Educational Philosophy at Western Kentucky University in Bowling Green, Kentucky.

The real heroes in "The Late, Great, Teacher Quit," as Constans and others came to call the walkout, were the striking teachers themselves. There have been thousands of teacher strikes in America over the last fifty years or so, but none of them came close to the scope and drama of the 1968 statewide Florida walkout. For one thing, the sheer magnitude of the venture was mind-boggling: 35,000 participants in 67 different counties spread across an entire state.

The hostile forces arrayed against FEA were daunting: county school districts, an entire state legislature, a volatile governor, an authoritative and powerful business cartel, and an apathetic public. Any one of these factors would have spelled serious trouble for an experienced, traditional union, but for an inexperienced and transitional organization like FEA to take them all on and survive is, to this day, amazing.

FEA's most formidable stumbling block, however, was none of the above. Its most obdurate and powerful opponent was the low tax culture of the state. It permeated everything, including the state's citizenry. It relegated public education to the depths of Florida's economic food chain, and made a mockery of the state's constitutional mandate of a quality public education for all citizens. Worst of all, few in political or business leadership positions cared.

Into that fearsome breach stepped the Florida Education Association and 35,000 courageous teachers. They may have been inexperienced, overmatched, and even naive, but they were not stupid or gullible. What Florida's teachers did in 1968 was most assuredly not comparable to Lord Cardigan's Charge of the Light Brigade in 1854 or the defense of Thermopoly Pass by King Leonidas and his Spartans in 480 B.C. However, for its time and place, what the teachers did was extraordinary and audacious.

The State of Florida's power structure took the measure of FEA and its membership, and the teachers withstood the test. Much was learned from the 1968 venture; it served as a matrix, good and bad, for rising teacher militancy across America.

Even looking back from today's vantage point, the statewide walkout was a seminal event in the history of Florida and the emergence of teacher unionism in America. When darkness descended on the Sunshine State, its teachers lit a torch and held it high for all to see.

NOTES

CHAPTER 1

1. United States Census Bureau, *1990 Census of Population and Housing*.
2. Stanley Smith, *Paper on Population Growth* (Gainesville: University of Florida, Bureau of Economic and Business Research).
3. Edmund Kallina, *Claude Kirk and the Politics of Confrontation* (Gainesville: University Press of Florida, 1993), p. 8.
4. Kallina, p. 14.
5. NEA Special Commission for Florida Study, NEA, 1966
6. NEA Special Commission for Florida Study, NEA, 1966.
7. Allan Morris, *The Florida Handbook* (Tallahassee, FL: Peninsular Publishing Co., 1973).

CHAPTER 2

1. Retired Living Information Center, State Taxes, 2008
2. Retired Living Information Center, State Taxes, 2008.
3. Retired Living Information Center, State Taxes, 2008.
4. Raymond Mason, *Dupont—The Man and His Family* (Oxford: Oxford University Press, 1990).

CHAPTER 3

1. Wade Hopping, interview appearing in James Cass, *Politics and Education* (Saturday Review, 1968), pp. 63–65.

2. Edmund Kallina, *Claude Kirk and the Politics of Confrontation* (Gainesville: University Press of Florida, 1993), p. 24.

3. Kallina, p. 77.

4. Kallina, p. 86.

5. "Ain't Nobody Gonna Touch King Claude," *Time* magazine, December 15, 1967.

6. Kallina, p. 77.

7. Kallina, p. 130.

8. Jan Godwin, "A Talk with Reuben Askew," *Research in Review* (1998): 1.

CHAPTER 4

1. FEA pamphlet, *Florida Under Sanctions*, 1968.

2. Anita Kumar, *St. Petersburg Times*, June 7, 2003.

3. NEA Special Commission Report, 1966.

4. NEA Special Commission Report, 1966.

5. Edmund Kallina, *Claude Kirk and the Politics of Confrontation* (Gainesville): University Press of Florida, 1993), p. 96.

6. "Strike in Pinellas," *St. Petersburg Times*, August 11, 1967.

7. Phil Constans, speech to Tangerine Bowl audience, FEA Archives.

CHAPTER 5

1. Interview with Mary Stanley, 2008.

2. Interview with Bea Griswold, 2008.

3. James Cass, "Politics and Education," *Saturday Review*, 1968.

4. Interview with Jim Geiger, 2007.

5. Robert Sanchez, "Special Session 1988 . . . and Special Session 1968 Statewide Teachers' Strike," Miami *Herald*, February 10, 1988.

CHAPTER 6

1. Author's observance and conversation, February 1968.

2. Interview with Rod Davis, former Sarasota County strike participant, 2008.

3. Interview with Barbara DeVane, former Suwannee County strike participant, 2008.

4. Jane Arnold, FEA website, home page. www.FEAWEB.org.

5. Edmund Kallina, *Claude Kirk and the Politics of Confrontation* (Gainesville: University Press of Florida, 1993), p. 101.

6. Don Treadwell, Pinellas County Teacher Association, posting on website. www.PCCTA.org.

7. James Kilpatrick, *Orlando Sentinel*, 1968.

8. James Cass, "Politics and Education in the Sunshine State," *Saturday Review* (1968): 76–79.

9. Phil Constans, letter (private), FEA Archives.

10. Interview with Ruth Holmes, 2008.

CHAPTER 7

1. Berkeley Miller and William Canak, "Porkchoppers to Lambchoppers," *Industrial and Labor Review* (January 1991): 349–66.

CHAPTER 8

1. Martin Waldron, "Students Backing Florida Teachers," *The New York Times*, February 21, 1967.

2. Berkeley Miller and William Canak, "Porkchoppers to Lambchoppers," *Industrial and Labor Review* (January 1991): 349–66.

3. Phil Constans, speech to Tangerine Bowl audience, FEA Archives.

CHAPTER 9

1. Interview with Jim Geiger, former Pasco County strike participant, 2008.

CHAPTER 10

1. NEA Procedings, 1968 Representative Assembly.

CHAPTER 11

1. Phil Constans, letter (personal), FEA Archives.

ABOUT THE AUTHOR

Born in Detroit, Michigan, **Don Cameron** was educated in Michigan's public schools, earned his bachelor's and master's degrees in education at Eastern Michigan University, did postgraduate work at the University of Michigan and New York University, and was awarded an honorary doctorate by Eastern Michigan University. He taught English and history at the secondary level in Birmingham, Michigan, before embarking on a long and varied career with the National Education Association, culminating in his tenure as executive director from 1983 to 2001.

While on the staff of the Michigan Education Association in 1968, he went to Florida for three weeks to assist the Florida Education Association with its statewide teacher walkout; he worked in Orange, Brevard, and Broward counties. Later, from 1976 to 1979, Cameron served as executive director of the Florida Teaching Profession–NEA, which was NEA's state affiliate in Florida at that time.

At the national level, Cameron was instrumental in the creation of the Learning First Alliance, a broad consortium of twelve national education associations, and cofounded the CEO Forum for Education Technology, a business/education partnership between the CEOs of twenty high-tech companies, the NEA, and the National School Boards Association. He has received numerous honors and awards, including the presidential Citizen's Medal, awarded by President Clinton, the highest national award given to an American civilian. He is also a charter member of the Eastern Michigan University Education Hall of Fame and has received an honorary fellowship from the Education Institute of Scotland, granted under a royal charter. He has been a member of the board of directors of many organizations, including People for the American Way, CEO Forum for Education, Princeton Review, Center for Policy Alternatives, National Democratic Institute for International Affairs (NDI), United Nations Association, Home and School Institute, and American Arbitration Association. Don Cameron lives in Arlington, Virginia, and Navarre Beach, Florida, with his wife, Ruth.